Emma Rose Barber

111 Churches
in London
That You
Shouldn't Miss

Photographs by Benedict Flett

emons:

For my brother Mark

MIX
Paper from
responsible sources
FSC® C043106

© Emons Verlag GmbH
All rights reserved
© Photographs by Benedict Flett, except:
Andy Bowden (St Mary's Harmondsworth) ch. 46;
John MacLean (St Augustine's, Hammersmith) ch. 45;
Theis and Khan (Lumen Chapel) ch. 9;
Kate Wilson for the photograph of *Stream*
(St Winifrede's Wimbledon), ch. 110
© Cover icon: shutterstock.com/mikecphoto
Layout: Eva Kraskes, based on a design
by Lübbeke | Naumann | Thoben
Maps: altancicek.design, www.altancicek.de
Basic cartographical information from Openstreetmap,
© OpenStreetMap-Mitwirkende, OdbL
Editing: Ros Horton
Printing and binding: Grafisches Centrum Cuno, Calbe
Printed in Germany 2020
ISBN 978-3-7408-0901-0
First edition

Did you enjoy this guidebook? Would you like to see more?
Join us in uncovering new places around the world on:
www.111places.com

Foreword

From Wanstead to Bermondsey, from Clapham Common to Stoke Newington, and Westminster to the City of London, this book takes you all over the capital to churches that are rarely visited. When I told people that I was writing this book, a common response was 'I didn't know there were that many churches in London'. London has as many as 4,000 churches! The guide has been written based on following the black marked crosses in a mini *A–Z* of London over the course of four years. Walking from church to church, ticking off the crosses as I went, resulted in many discoveries, and without spending any money.

These buildings can be places of quiet, although sometimes you hear music, and they are often bathed in stunning light and playful shadow. The churches provide another way of looking at London's history, and reveal their own turbulent histories with fires, bombs and changes in religious practice. There are paintings, furnishings and memorials to figures such as John Donne. There are columns and capitals, vaults and arches, fonts and pulpits, showing you centuries of skill and labour that went into making these buildings.

Gaze at gigantic Egyptian-like statues of animals, a naked Madonna, monuments to merchant adventurers who collected bodies for the British Museum, little statuettes of forgotten women in history, images of St Veronica who wiped the brow of Christ as he staggered up the hill to Calvary with his cross; or, the raw, red carving of the Devil dripping with blood. There are churches with surviving medieval foundations, remains of monasteries, chapels belonging to almshouses, the church made in the Brutalist style, or a hollowed-out shell, containing the most romantic garden you will find in London. There are churches with cafés in them and those that have exciting contemporary art displayed within.

The guide encourages you to look up, look down and look all around, both inside and out.

Emma Rose Barber

111 Churches

1 St Cyprian Clarence Gate

Romantic medievalising in a 19th-century church

A church that could be mistaken for something built in 1342, and yet it was not consecrated until 1903. The Scottish-born architect, Sir Ninian Comper (1864–1960) was alive to the Oxford Movement, which sought to bring back a pre-Reformation feel to the liturgy and design of churches. The idea was to abandon the classical style that had become the norm for most 18th-century (now Protestant) churches, and so expose the aesthetic tug of war between the classical and the Gothic (associated with Catholic Britain). After all, Gothic was 'here first'. So, vaults, buttresses and pointed arches, medieval colour, decoration and mood returned. Here is Comper's result with the distinctive rood screen.

And while medieval church design became fashionable once again, it became all right to burn incense, even kiss the Crucifix and readopt ancient rules and rituals. A unique thing about this church is that Comper designed everything himself; he was the true interior designer with vision, as well as being the architect. See the extra ornamentation that previously would not have been allowed: the curtains around the altar, the roof with carved flowers and coloured angels. Yet when it was first built, the church's design must have been received negatively by those familiar with the cool and light and white classicising features of 18th-century London churches – those designed by Nicholas Hawksmoor or Sir Christopher Wren for example.

St Cyprian was a 3rd-century Archbishop of Carthage, known to be a good public speaker. A carefree youth, he ended up as a condemned prisoner in 258CE, leading to his execution. His relics are allegedly in places such as Lyons, Arles and Venice, but there are none in Baker Street. With its sense of openness, the architect was no doubt thinking about how words spoken and sung could echo around the arches and spaces of Cyprian's church.

Address Glentworth Street, NW1 6AX, +44 (0)207 723 0426, www.stcyprians.weebly.com | Getting there Tube to Baker Street (Circle, Hammersmith & City and Metropolitan Lines); bus: 139 or 189 | Hours Check first with the administrator: stcyprianscg@gmail.com | Tip You are not far from Madame Tussauds, but there is no replica of Comper there. You can see a portrait of him at the National Portrait Gallery (though closed until 2023).

2 St Mary

Modern architecture adapts to the medieval

The church is situated not far from the River Thames and near Barnes Pond, where you can watch the ducks. The church is striking for the architectural juxtaposition of old foundations, such as the Norman porch, and the rugged rendering of flint, stone and brick with a mainly modern interior. There is one chapel that remains of Norman heritage (note the narrow lancet, slightly pointed windows above the altar), dedicated to Stephen Langton (c. 1150–1228), archbishop of Canterbury from 1207 until his death. He consecrated St Mary's on his way back from Runnymede after imploring King John to sign the *Magna Carta* (15 June, 1215). Look closely for some ruled ochre lines, behind a layer of stone wall: the remains of medieval wall paintings. Do not miss the tiny figurine in a robe and bare feet attached to a column. His left arm is up as if to bless, suggesting it might be Christ.

A dreadful fire destroyed the interior in 1978, but it was restored and completed in 1984. You now see a stunning space, the timber roof visible from the exterior, creating a canopy over the open plan, which emphasises not only light, but how a congregation can be together in one unified place. The work was designed by the architect Edward Cullinan (1931–2019). He was educated at Queens' College, Cambridge, and later designed buildings for the University, such as the Centre for Mathematical Sciences. He had a huge portfolio ranging from the gateway to Petra to Winchester College Arts Centre.

The church also has a garden, with a glorious border of shrubs and flowers in high summer. Although the exterior of the church is Victorian Gothic, the graveyard has many substantial tombs in it, from the 16th to 18th centuries. So, the building and the exterior space give you a useful visual and documentary survey of how churches show bits and pieces, fragments and stones from all periods in history.

Address Church Road, Barnes, SW13 9HL, +44 (0)208 741 5422, www.stmarybarnes.org | Getting there Mainline to Barnes (South Western) or Barnes Bridge (South Western); bus: 33, 72, 209 or 485 | Hours Daily 9am – 3.30pm | Tip There are plenty of good walks in the vicinity – by the Thames or on Barnes Common.

3__ St Mary

Spot Turner painting the river

A picture-perfect church, beside the River Thames. The only feature separating you from the water are some houseboats and in the churchyard the house boats' letter boxes, attached to the trees as if they were bird boxes. On the far bank, near where the late-Victorian artist J. M. Whistler (1834–1903) painted, and where the painter J. M. W. Turner (1775–1851) lived, you can see old wharves and buildings, now smart riverside flats. By the church, ducks dabble, gabble and graze. Turner painted the church in c. 1797 with his consummate skill in combining space and perspective with a sense of atmosphere. We see the church on the horizon, with a cluster of buildings on the north side of the river to the left, and Battersea Bridge in the background. Turner did not bring the light out in this work; after all, atmosphere is what matters, but when the sunlight is on the church, it can look quite stunning.

The current building was completed in 1777, by Joseph Dixon, although it has foundations reaching back as far as the 8th century. This is an elegant brick-faced church with a brick tower interfaced with white stone quoins rising into the sky, only blocked by all the modern flats that have been built in recent years, making the church's position there extremely precious. The church's façade consists of the pedimented portico broken up by the west entrance door and a slightly bowed window at the front.

Inside there is a modern stained glass window dedicated to Turner by John Hayward (along with three others, 1976–82), which shows the well-known self-portrait Turner painted when he was a young man. And the church has a special chair that he painted in. Other windows commemorate William Curtis (1746–99), demonstrator of Botany at what is now called the Chelsea Physic Garden, and the 'visionary' artist William Blake, who married Catherine Boucher in the church.

Address Battersea Church Road, Battersea, SW11 3NA, +44 (0)207 228 9648, www.stmarysbattersea.org.uk | **Getting there** Tube to Clapham Junction (Circle, District, Northern and Victoria Lines); bus: 19, 49, 170, 219, 319 or 345 | **Hours** Mon–Fri 10am–noon | **Tip** Nearby is the sculpture department of the Royal College of Art, which welcomes visitors during their summer degree shows. There are also many interesting river walks to be had in the area.

4__ St Mary

Dazzling decoration and colour

On the exterior, a masculine, muscular church, entered through a striking polygonal porch, designed by H. S. Goodhart-Rendel (1887–1959). There is a lot of red brick at this church, and it probably feels more Arts and Crafts, and less Victorian Gothic, even though it is a 19th-century church. Inside, the mood changes. One of the notable features is a painted screen behind two pilasters of the *Deposition*, where we see Mary holding up her son. To the right an angel faces in another direction, while his body is twisted to his left, shying away from what is unfolding before him. To the left, an angel kneels to witness the event.

Against the brick on a wall to the left and easily missed in this rather dark, but beautifully illuminated church, is a thin, wiry structure cascading down intertwining petal and flower forms, curves, volutes and curls, where at the top is a cross. Hidden within is a bell. One solitary bell to which is attached a long metal rope. This is the church's Arts and Crafts bell, lovingly carved out of metal. It could have been wrenched out of a fiery furnace and made crisp from real leaves thrown into the fire, which then become covered in the metal to make forms from nature for posterity. And then in a part of the church known as the apse, you will see the *Visitation*, the narrative scene recorded in *Luke* (1: 36–56), when John the Baptist's mother Elizabeth comes to greet Mary when they have both heard about their respective pregnancies.

The interior is built in the model of a Romanesque interior – in addition to early English modelled Gothic arches and round headed arches as well as pointed windows above. There are many details to admire, for example, a colonnade of simple stone breaking into brick mouldings, with pictures in the spandrels of the arches. Here is a sturdy form of Victorian medievalising to love and admire or denounce and decry.

Address 30 Bourne Street, SW1W 8JJ, +44 (0)207 730 9719, www.stmarysbournest.com | Getting there Tube to Sloane Square (Circle and District Lines), Victoria, (Circle, District and Victoria Lines), Pimlico (Victoria Line); bus: 11, 81, 137, 170, 350, 452, C1 or U3 | Hours Fri 9.30am–4pm or Sun at service times | Tip The church is a 5-minute walk from Holy Trinity, Sloane Street (see ch. 86).

5 Bermondsey Abbey
The place that marks the spot

In some editions of the mini *A to Z*, black crosses are marked on the pages that represent churches. Marking these crosses with a circle was the means by which the churches for this book were chosen. Phyllis Isobella Pearsall (1906–96), the author and designer of the *A to Z*, tramped many more miles than I have to complete her book, and is an unsung hero. Of course, the black cross does not necessarily mean an open and thriving church. It can mean something that used to exist. A black cross on the page for this site marks the location of an old abbey, but which is currently a large car-free square, a place for enjoyment and leisure.

The area now has a hotel, a bar cum cinema and about three or four cafés, where once might have been a cloister, or a chapter house. The blue plaque marking the site says that the abbey was founded as a Priory of the Order of Cluny (1082–1537) by Alwyn Child, the last date telling us so much about the fate of British abbeys and monasteries in the 16th century. The house here was granted to Sir Robert Southwell in 1541 and he then sold it to a Sir Thomas Pope who pulled down most of the buildings and built himself a new residence. Clearly, he was not partial to ecclesiastical ruins, as there are none left.

In the heyday of the priory's existence, there were also abbots living in houses from St Augustine's of Canterbury in Tooley Street. All good monks need beverages, and we know that they ran a tavern in Rotherhithe Street, part of which was built on piles. Now, the laity are back to walk on those once hallowed stones, but with the promise of a café as the elixir of life, rather than through the conduit of a priest's words. And instead of miracle crosses dug up from the Thames (according to the legend, in 1117 the *Rood of Grace* was found nearby having dropped from heaven, attracting many pilgrims), coffee is now the new wonder instant cure.

Address Bermondsey Square, SE1 3UN, www.bermondseysquare.net | Getting there
Mainline to London Bridge (Southeastern); Tube to Bermonsdey (Jubilee Line), London
Bridge (Jubilee and Northern Lines); bus: 42, 188 or C10 | Hours Accessible 24 hours | Tip
Cafés and shops in Bermondsey Street, also the church of St Mary Magdalen (see ch. 6).

6 St Mary Magdalen
The site of a monastery church

St Mary Magdalen was the monastery church for Bermondsey Abbey (see ch. 5). But nothing structural remains of the monastery, as is the way with British monastic institutions, when their turbulent, historical fate was destruction. For now, though, we have the church as living evidence of an interesting building history in this area. Although the present church dates only as far back as 1680, the tower is dated to the medieval period and you will recognise a Gothic-styled west front. So, the church is quite an architectural hotchpotch! Then again, we will get quite used to this model with London churches.

On the church's exterior is a rather charming inscription that reads: *This church is open for divine service on Sundays at 11.30 and at half past 6 o'clock and for churchings and baptisms at 4 o'clock. The sacrament of the Lord's supper is administered on the first Sunday in each month.* The announcement is signed by Lewes Tugwell. The word 'churching' relates to the time when a woman, having given birth, makes her first public appearance at church.

Inside, you might like to see the entry in the church register to James Herriott, married on 4 January, 1624–25, 'one of the 40 children of his father, a Scotchman'. Another object that belongs to the church (but currently at the V&A museum) is a silver alms dish – the *Bermondsey Mazer*, which is thought to be the only surviving piece of silver from the Bermondsey Abbey collections. A mazer, quite often made of maple wood, is a drinking bowl, and monks often had their own, as well as communal ones for visitors. The fact that this one was silver suggests the monastery had been rich.

Behind the church building is a large garden where tombs and gravestones lie. Now it is a people's park both for the dead and the living, as it is clearly being used for lunchtime sandwich eating and lounging on the grass.

Address 193 Bermondsey Street, SE1 3UW, +44 (0)207 234 0100, www.stmarysbermondsey.org.uk | Getting there Mainline to London Bridge (Southeastern); Tube to London Bridge (Jubilee and Northern Lines); bus: 188 or C10 | Hours Fri 11am–2pm | Tip The church is very close to Bermondsey Abbey Square (see ch. 5) and the White Cube Gallery in Bermondsey Street (www.whitecube.com).

7 St Matthew

What wonders can be done out of destruction

The sad fate of a church's history can be turned around, as we see at St Matthew's. Together with many other East End churches, it was bombed in the Blitz. Little was left standing, but now it has a cool, robust, in places brutal, but stylish early 1960s interior. Upstairs in a chapel overlooking the large nave from which double doors open up to view it below, are paintings dedicated to the Virgin Mary, done in a strikingly angular Cubist style. Downstairs, along the walls, are some beautifully carved relief sculptures of the *Stations of the Cross*, done by Don Potter (d. 2004). The artist was trained by Eric Gill and these are powerful carvings. There is one in particular, which stands out for variation on a theme. Christ is struggling along, bearing his cross, and above and beside him stands a woman, with two young girls looking on. A signal that children too bear witness to suffering. Admire the bold high relief on the staircase, a sculpture of St Michael lancing and tramping the Devil in one forceful move.

If the area still feels rather rural, that's because it has a rural past – as originally there were marshes and woods here. It is a peaceful sanctuary, but a church with a vigorous and torturous history. The building was one of 12 churches (known as the 12 Apostles) built in what was hitherto a poor area of the East End in the 18th century. A recurring image in the church is of the blind beggar, although this has a medieval root related to the nobleman Sir Henry de Montfort (1238–65), who fought at the Battle of Evesham in 1265, where he was victorious. All well and good, until, according to one legend, he lost his sight, and became a poor beggar to fund the nuptials of his beautiful daughter. Look out for London pubs called 'The Blind Beggar'. In the late 19th century, owing to philanthropic, progressive views, the church gained a reputation for its Christian socialism.

Address St Matthew's Row, E2 6DT, +44 (0)207 739 7586, www.st-matthews.co.uk |
Getting there Overground to Shoreditch High Street; Tube to Bethnal Green (Central
Line); bus: 8 or 388 | Hours Daily 8.30am–6pm | Tip Brick Lane and all its junk shops
and stalls, as well as numerous restaurants and bars, including the legendary Brick Lane
Beigel Bake, are close.

8__Fitzrovia Chapel
An old hospital chapel

To look after the sick, needy, poor and old was an ancient Christian duty. Although hospitals have always existed, in the Middle Ages it was recognised that the likelihood of a physical cure was remote. You would go to be healed spiritually and prepare yourself for death. Even today, we can see old hospital chapels that would originally have been attached to either a hospital and / or a monastery.

Consider the Fitzrovia Chapel, through a pedestrian area flanked by apartments, which is the only part left of the old Middlesex Hospital. It was designed by John Loughborough Pearson (1817–97) who also designed St Augustine's Kilburn (see ch. 60) as seen on the panel dedicated to him in the vestibule to the chapel (11 December, 1897) and one to his son – Frank L. Pearson (1864–1947), the overseer of the project. Although this does not have a medieval foundation, the hospital's origins date back to the 18th century; it was established expressly for the poor.

A few years back most of the hospital was demolished so as to build smart new housing. The chapel has been kept and turned into an arts venue, making it accessible. The space is stunning: colourful, ornate, glistening with gold and many veins of marble, with different surfaces and textures of paint and mosaic on every available surface. A reference to the frail is found in the stained glass windows designed by the legendary Victorian firm, Clayton and Bell. Other memorials to people who contributed to the hospital over the years include one to Diana Beck (1902–56), a neurosurgeon and the first 'medical woman on the staff of this hospital'.

Even though the chapel is a small space, an area was designated for the Baptistry where you can still see the font and an inscription on a pillar, telling you that it was dedicated to John Bland Sutton, a surgeon at the hospital. There is an inscription to this effect in the stained glass window here.

Address Fitzroy Place, 2 Pearson Square, W1T 3BF, +44 (0)203 409 9895, www.fitzroviachapel.org | Getting there Tube to Tottenham Court Road (Central and Northern Lines), Goodge Street (Northern Line), Warren Street (Victoria Line); bus: 14, 55, 98, 159 or 453 | Hours Wed 11am–4pm | Tip The chapel is not far from the Cartoon Museum and another church built in the style of the Oxford Movement – All Saints, Margaret Street.

9 Lumen United Reformed
'Lumen' light is captivating

From immigrants' chapel with the liturgy in the Gaelic language, to a modern church, which has recently had the most stunning remodelling out of a 1960s interior (Theis and Khan 2007–08). The architects were also asked to design a space for classrooms, meeting rooms and café, visible from the street. Lumen is now more than just a church and is a showcase for cutting-edge design, making the best of the natural daylight. Here you will find a cool contemporary interior amidst Georgian Bloomsbury houses, which contributes to an interesting contrast, particularly as you enter from the north and move towards a light-filled garden. The place demonstrates just what flexible spaces churches can be for contemporary art and architecture.

The church is a roll call of all that is tactile, sensuous and substantial. Here are just some: at the centre of the church interior is a conical shell-like construction, 36 feet (11 metres) in height to a single rooflight. It is known as the shaft of light, and makes the space accessible to all faiths. Look at the Rona Smith geometric screen, which is also the north window, facing onto the street. The spiralling shapes means you are not looking at the illusion of a window, but a real one, essentially a work of art. And then there are the font, drinking fountain and garden fountain by the Turner Prize nominee Alison Wilding, where smooth materials make perfect receptacles for water.

The stained glass window, made of 1,000 pieces of glass, is all hand-cut. It was designed by Pierre Fourmaintraux (1966). The surface of the glass is chipped, so that when the sunlight appears, a dazzling effect is particularly intense. Unusually, the glass is set into concrete panels, a French technique dating to the 1920s and introduced to this country by the artist.

The first minister of the church (from 1818), James Boyd, baptised John Ruskin in 1819.

Address 88 Tavistock Place, WC1H 9RS, +44 (0)207 833 1080, www.lumenurc.org.uk | **Getting there** Mainline to King's Cross and St Pancras (many lines); Tube to King's Cross/ St Pancras International (Circle, Hammersmith & City and Northern Lines), Russell Square (Piccadilly Line); bus: 10, 17, 45, 46, 59, 68, 91 or 168 | **Hours** Sun noon – 5pm, also at times when café is open, Mon – Fri 8am – 4.30pm | **Tip** The church is located close to the delightful Foundling Museum, dedicated to foundlings in the 18th century, where both Handel and the artist Hogarth were philanthropically involved (www.foundlingmuseum.org.uk).

10__ St George

The epitome of classical architecture

A mini classical temple that you might think belongs more to ancient Athens than contemporary London. A mini version of the British Museum, which is moments away, just north of the church. It is quite difficult to appreciate this beautiful Hawksmoor-designed façade, as it is located on a busy road. The best view is at the back of the church (first right from Museum Street to the left). Here, you will also get a much better view of the tower, which is effectively an icon to George I (1660–1727), but which looks like an Egyptian pyramid. Look right to the top and behold, who do you see? Although it was paid for by an MP called William Hucks, his primary job was 'Royal Brewer'. So, a London church tower with a difference, and a frothy twist. The stone carver Tim Crawley redesigned the original lions and unicorns around the base of the tower, symbols of the United Kingdom, used by the Hanoverian monarch, and in the rhyme – 'The lion and the unicorn were fighting for the crown'.

The façade consists of columns on bases, Corinthian capitals and steps up to a portico, topped by a triangular pediment. However, you cannot enter the church, as you might expect, from the west, due to it being on a narrow site. Originally, this church's orientation inside was south–north (where the altar was), when the ideal is west–east. But recent restoration has put it back to west–east (where the altar is), with the apse, even though you still enter from the south.

Inside, though, the church feels like a Greek cross plan, all equal parts and symmetrical. And the light inside, even on a grey day, is still crystal clear and bright. A way to decide whether an architect is any good or not, is to see how they deal with light.

The church is close to other classical stars, such as the Elgin marbles at the British Museum. Anthony Trollope, the novelist, was baptised here in 1815.

Address Bloomsbury Way, High Holborn, WC1A 2SA, +44 (0)207 242 1979, www.stgeorgesbloomsbury.org.uk | Getting there Crossrail to Tottenham Court Road; Tube to Tottenham Court Road (Central and Northern Lines), Holborn (Central and Piccadilly Lines); bus: 1, 29, 38, 98 or 168 | Hours Wed 1.30–3.30pm (some weeks), Thu 1–3pm (every 2nd week), Fri 1.30–3.30pm, Sun noon–1pm | Tip Leave plenty of time to visit the British Museum.

11 __ St Mary with St George

A cute German Lutheran church

This church is in Sandwich Street. There is a 'greasy spoon' café at one end of the street, but no sandwich shop as such. Although, it is close to St Pancras International where you can take the high speed to the Kentish town of Sandwich. An anecdote records how John Montagu, 4th Earl of Sandwich (a nominal title), was given two pieces of bread with a piece of meat between them, as he did not want to leave the gambling table.

This is a street, paved on one side, not with gold, but light. It contains Georgian houses and university accommodation. The church does not have a majestic tower, steeple, or obvious main façade with central door. This is a no-fuss church. There is a glass doorway, as if it is the entrance to offices.

Words are inscribed above the glass entrance, replete with a cross attached. To the right, is a free-standing cross, embedded in white rocks acting as a supportive base for the cross rising up, or standing for the jagged edges and rocks of the hill of Golgotha.

Other than the cross, the only sign that this is a church is a little panel behind glass, to the left of the doorway, which is the church noticeboard. Through the glass door is a little vase of flowers. An unintentional choreographed play perhaps on glass and reflection and illusion?

Look through the glass panel, through the glass vase to see the reflection of the wooden cross behind you. This may be a simple church, but slowly, slowly it reveals itself and even though you might not go inside, what you see is beautifully adequate. There is an aesthetically pleasing inscription, carved out of wood on another board with the words 'St Mary's, German Lutheran Church'. A church that seems to live up to what Martin Luther (1483–1546) urged: plain speaking, authenticity and the plain, original gospel truth. Like Luther, the Word is all that this place needs.

Address 10 Sandwich Street, WC1H 9PL, +44 (0)27 383 2146, www.london-ost.german-church.org | **Getting there** Tube to King's Cross, (Hammersmith & City, Metropolitan, Northern, Piccadilly and Victoria Lines); bus: 59, 73, 91, 390 or 476 | **Hours** Open on Sun for services, or daily for the exterior | **Tip** The Petrie Museum of Egyptian Archaeology is close by, in Malet Place.

12___St Pancras and Crypt Gallery

Classical statues and contemporary art

The four *caryatids*, still and serene, but dirty and somewhat ignored, face the Marylebone Road and mark the spot. St Pancras (architects William and Henry Inwood, 1819–22) looks like a temple, and is thought to be based on the Ionic temple of Erechtheum and the Tower of the Winds in Athens. It is best to try and imagine that you are on a hill in Greece looking at the building, surrounded by olive groves and statues. The *caryatids* have fluted drapes about them and hold torches and vessels, as if poised to pour oil or water on the passing cars. But, in fact, this relates to their position by the burial chamber in the crypt space; its structure being supported by the *caryatids*, as this is a space for art exhibitions. Its nooks, crannies and crevices provide a wonderful space for creativity. So, the muses are still here, even if the Gods are not.

The west end of the church is not on the main road, but on Upper Woburn Place. There is a classical portico with Ionic capitals and six fluted columns to mark your arrival.

St Pancratius was martyred and beheaded in 304CE, when just a mere boy, by the Roman Emperor Diocletian. But he did then become the patron saint of children. Left an orphan, he was brought up by his uncle, but was ordered to worship Roman gods. As a result of his refusal, as is the case with many early Christian fighters for the new belief, he was sentenced to death. It is believed that when St Augustine came to England from Rome to evangelise those 'Angles' whom Gregory had seen in the Rome market believing they were 'angels', he had some St Pancras relics in his travelling satchel. There is another Roman connection, as an ancient church existed on this site previously, overlooking the River Fleet, where there was a Roman encampment.

Address Euston Road, NW1 2BA, +44 (0)20 7388 1461, www.cryptgallery.org | Getting there Mainline to King's Cross (LNER) and St Pancras International (Southeastern and Thameslink); Tube to Euston (Hammersmith & City Line), King's Cross (Circle, Metropolitan, Northern, Piccadilly and Victoria Lines); bus: 59, 68, 91 or 168 | Hours Mon–Thu 8am–6pm, Sun 7.30–11.30am, 5.30–7pm | Tip The church is situated close to the British Library, the national library of the United Kingdom (www.bl.uk).

13__St Paul
Brutal and beautiful

If you wonder what the Brutalist style (c. 1950s – 70s) is, this church might just show you. While, when it was first rebuilt in 1958 – 60, it might have seemed very different from what was there before, its layout harks back to early Christian building styles.

The interior plan of the church is striking: it is in the form of a Greek cross where you can see all the sides of the church, with the altar in the middle. This was seen as the ideal design during the Italian Renaissance, when the saying 'man is the measure of all things' was also a call to church architects to make a church layout seem equal and balanced. The priest would be presiding over the liturgy and the Eucharist from a central position; that is, at the centre, where all four arms of the cross meet. Here, the altar is on a low dais, ennobling it, but not creating a big distance between the priest and the congregation.

The whole space feels unified and communal.

The exterior is jagged with sharp edged parts: the triangle shape is repeated in different ways, as a rhythm of repeating angles overhanging the bricked wall and abutting the brick pitched roof. At the top is a glass structure framed by a striking red band. The entrance is a simple post and lintel system, no classicising columns here. On the lintel, essentially above the doorway, is bright red lettering announcing the entrance and function of the church.

At the time, cutting-edge materials were used: a concrete floor, woodwork tiles in the ceiling and bare brickwork. Charles Lutyens, the great-nephew of the architect Edwin Lutyens, designed the mosaics that you see on the walls inside (1963 – 68). The church, probably seen as quite shocking at first, is functional, easy to use and devoid of Victorian trimmings and accessories, which had become the norm for many London churches prior to the war. Now, it seems refreshing and honest.

Address Burdett Road, Bow, E3 4AR, +44 (0)203 774 6833,
www.stpaulsbowcommon.org.uk | **Getting there** Tube to Mile End (Central Line;
DLR to Westferry; bus: 277, 309, D6 or D7 | **Hours** Mon–Wed & Fri 8am–4pm, Sun
11.30am–4pm | **Tip** The church is situated not far from The Museum of the Book,
dedicated to exhibits of Bibles and other related printed and illuminated manuscript
material (www.churchofthebook.com/museum).

14__St Wilfrid

Visible World War II damage

This is a church named after St Wilfrid (633 – 709), born in Northumbria and whose cult was based in Ripon.

A church tucked into the north edge of a pretty residential square. Many parts of the building date back to World War II damage, still to be undone. It is difficult for churches to restore and maintain their buildings, even over a long period of time as there are constant demands on structure, stone, brick, tower and pillar. A poignant inscription plaque says the church opened with a blessing during World War I (1915) but was wrecked with a bomb in World War II in 1940. Restored, though, so it says 'happily'. Here is tangible evidence of how the plight of war and fervent faith can come together.

You will know you are in a Catholic church when you see the Virgin Mary; her blue robe pushed back to reveal a camel colour underdress. About her waist, is a glitzy gold belt, dazzling alongside the copper underside of her blue garment. She is elegantly dressed. Her hands are splayed out downwards like her head. At the high altar, there are a lot of visual distractions: lace, the gilded lily, polished gold candlesticks, painted surfaces, a bold red border, extravagant gold wings of angels' glorying gowns, the purple passion cloth of Bishopric status covering the tabernacle at the centre; marble, surface, and a lit candle.

Note the reliefs of the *Road to Calvary*. Here are soldiers, mourners and weepers in woollen stockings, short robed, tense and taut arm muscles, body suits showing their musculature, the bodies bending and supporting themselves as they carry the weight of Jesus collapsing under his cross. These Calvary scenes are numbered; you can marvel at Roman numerals while looking at the polished, fine, angular facial features of these Cavaliers. There is a compliant and serene horse as well.

Note, too, the glass door saying Confessional and Crying Chapel.

Address Lorrimore Road, SE17 3LZ, +44 (0)207 358 4259, www.swkp.org.uk | Getting there Tube to Kennington or Oval (Northern Line); bus: 143, 155 or P5 | Hours Daily | Tip The church is close to Kennington Park and Bee Urban – a social enterprise dedicated to promoting urban beekeeping, horticulture and community growing.

15 St Pancras Old Church

The tomb of Sir John Soane and a mortuary

The Midland Railway tried to build a tunnel through the church-yard in the 1860s, but this caused havoc with buried bodies and was debated at the House of Commons. Apart from its pretty location and proportions in an unprepossessing area, this church has many interesting historical connections. Joseph Grimaldi, a clown, married here in 1801. Mary Wollstonecraft, who, pregnant (with Mary Shelley), by William Godwin was married here in 1797, only to be buried herself in the churchyard by the end of the year.

Beside the tree, is the burial site of the legendary architect, Sir John Soane (1753–1837), who designed the Bank of England and many other London buildings. His tomb here is a small architectural wonder. His monument was eventually carried out by George Gilbert Scott (1811–78) in the 19th century, in a style true to what Soane had believed in throughout his career as an architect: that the classical language of architecture is supreme. So, into eternity he went with his beloved classical model; even at death he practised what he had preached!

It is also worth seeing the colourful mosaic design on the tall obelisk-like structure acting as a sundial. This was designed by and dedicated to Baroness Burdett Coutts (as in the bankers), who designed a model estate at Holly Village, Highgate. She also invented drinking fountains for dogs, which Soane would have approved of, as he and his wife were utterly devoted to theirs.

What you see of the church today is largely Victorian; it is delicate and small and with an entrance portal of faux dentilled Romanesque decoration. The church is perhaps one of the earliest Christian sites in London. It was one of the favourites of Elizabeth I and she continued to allow Latin mass here after the Reformation. Indeed, it was throughout history a place of Catholic safety, and many escapees from the French Revolution are buried here.

Address Pancras Road, NW1 1UL, +44 (0)207 424 0724, www.posp.co.uk/st-pancras-old-church | **Getting there** Mainline to King's Cross (East Coast Mainline), St Pancras International (Thameslink, East Midlands Trains and Southeastern); Tube to King's Cross (Hammersmith & City, Northern, Piccadilly and Victoria Lines); bus: 46 or 214 | **Hours** Daily 9.30am – 3pm | **Tip** The church is located very near to the Regent's Canal and the Camley Street Natural Park.

16_ St Luke with Holy Trinity
A village church with murder at its heart

Many men and women have been murdered throughout history. Spencer Perceval's (1762–1812) claim to fame is that he has (so far), been the only prime minister who has been shot and killed in the House of Commons in Westminster.

At this church, in the heart of Charlton village in south-east London, is a bust to this man (made by Sir Francis Chantrey), with an inscription beneath. He had been prime minister for three years before he died. He began his career in the Law and was at Lincoln's Inn (see ch. 49, where there is another inscription to him). The connection to Charlton is personal in that he rented a house here with his brother, and they respectively fell in love with two sisters – who just happened to live in their old home! One wonders if there was a strategy to their courtships.

John Bellingham, a merchant, murdered Perceval as he entered the lobby of the House of Commons on the evening of 11 May, 1812. He seems to have had a grievance against the government. But his requests were rejected, and as a result he took things into his own hands. Perceval left a wife and 12 children and is buried beneath the church.

Other than this commemoration, the church is full of many ancient memorials, inscriptions, cartouches and stone plaques. There are many dedicated to the local landowning Maryon-Wilson family, who lived for a time at Charlton House, opposite the church – a beautiful Jacobean house, begun in 1612 for Sir Adam Newton. There is also one to Anne Boleyn and Edward Wilkinson, Yeoman of the Mouth to Henry VIII, which as you may have guessed is a post dedicated to providing the monarch's food.

Constructed of red brick, the church itself has a rounded Netherlandish gable over the porch. The paths with old graves feel a bit wonky, but contribute to a distinctive atmosphere.

Address The Village, SE7 8UG, +44 (0)7922 587 263, www.charlton.church | Getting there Mainline to Charlton (Southeastern), then walk up Charlton Church Lane; bus: 486 passes the door | Hours Wed 10.30am–noon and on Sun mornings around service times | Tip Across the road is Charlton House, a stunning Jacobean mansion, which has a café, an Italian restaurant and some attractive gardens (www.greenwichheritage.org). You might also like to visit The Village Green Grocers directly opposite the church – a wonderful resource of provisions, which won the 2020 Best of Greenwich High Street Retailer award.

17__St Michael and All Angels

Arts and Crafts meets Catholic revival

How can you miss a church close to one of the most beautiful garden suburbs of London? This is the Bedford Park Estate (begun 1876), with the church (begun 1879) situated at its southern edge. There are elegant red-brick houses with white painted gates, and each one is slightly different. To go there is to arouse envy, which may not be a good thing. The exterior of the church, with the contrast of red brick and white joinery mirrors the houses and is all pink and green within, replicating the plant border by the exterior in the church garden. The church was built by Richard Norman Shaw (1831–1912) in the Arts and Crafts style. The rood screen with the *Crucifixion*, and the statues of Mary and John the Evangelist, was a common structure in the church prior to the Reformation, when churches in England were Catholic. The screen was a dividing structure, often with statues on top to separate choir (where the monks sat) and congregation, but which were also symbolic in a sort of you-and-them scenario. Late 19th-century architects such as Sir Ninian Comper brought back these screens when Catholicism had a revival; a wonderful riposte to an edict ordering the dismantling of 'rood lofts' in 1559 under the reign of Queen Elizabeth I.

One striking feature is a painting of the *Visitation* (1922), a well-known image of the Middle Ages and Renaissance periods. This narrates the moment when Elizabeth, the future mother of John the Baptist, who had been barren, celebrates the news of her impending birth with the much younger Mary, the soon-to-be mother of Jesus. As is habitual, the scene shows them embracing. It is fun to work out which is Elizabeth, and which is Mary. The clue lies in the fact that Elizabeth, as an older kinswoman to Mary, usually looks older! Sometimes we see their husbands lurking behind. Not that they had much to do with these conceptions!

Address Bath Road, W4 1TT, +44 (0)208 994 1380, www.smaaa.org.uk/wp | **Getting there** Tube to Turnham Green (District Line); bus: 94, 272 or E3 | **Hours** Daily 9am–5pm and at service times | **Tip** The London Buddhist Vihara, a centre for Theravada Buddhism, is at 17 The Avenue. Open daily to visitors, they run a regular programme of events (www.londonbuddhistvihara.org).

18 All Hallows by the Tower

Coffee by the river and wonderful art

This church is a visual encyclopaedia of building styles: Roman, Anglo-Saxon, Perpendicular Gothic, the 17th century, and now the 21st century. It is easy to miss these stylistic creases and collisions. Yet any church building is always in flux. And like so many City churches, All Hallows was virtually destroyed by a bomb in 1940. In 1666, Sir Christopher Wren (1632–1723) also watched the Great Fire spreading madly and wantonly from a tower to the side of this church.

Aside from styles, there are magical combinations of materials and textures in brick and stone. There are angels on the waves on exterior carvings; in spring there is blossom in the small churchyard and coffee brews in the café right beside the church. And from the church you can see the Tower of London.

Look at the 16th-century memorial to the merchant Hieronimus Benalius, an Italian, of Seething Lane (d. 1538) and where the great 17th-century diarist Samuel Pepys lived for a while. Another historic European connection is seen in the triptych, the Tate Panel, probably Flemish, early 16th century. Four saints including John the Baptist protect the possible patron of the work, Mr Tate. St Jerome is there with his characteristic cardinal's hat, and St Joseph is on the right, wearing platform shoes known as 'pattens' (see ch. 31). The shoes might represent his travelling status, as soon after the birth of Christ, the family escaped to Egypt, where they fled from King Herod.

At the high altar is a *Last Supper* (1957), by Brian Thomas. Christ is standing (unusual), one apostle stands to the right (covering half his head with his right hand), another apostle to the left is on his knees putting out his hands to receive the wafer. But where is Judas? This is the quintessential modern image of the Last Supper. No sinner is obviously present at the table. Christ is blessing all, for us all.

Address Byward Street, EC3R 5BJ, +44 (0)207 481 2928, www.ahbtt.org.uk | Getting there Tube to Tower Hill (Circle and District Lines); DLR to Tower Gateway; bus: 15, 42, 78 or 100; river boat to Tower Pier | Hours Apr–Oct Mon–Fri 8am–6pm, Sat & Sun 10am–5pm; Nov–Mar Mon–Fri 8am–5pm, Sat & Sun 10am–5pm | Tip The church also has a charming museum, with fragments and objects from its past. This takes you into the crypt as well. The church is situated moments from the Tower of London.

19___Charterhouse Chapel
A place for brothers and sisters

The chapel is part of the 7-acre complex that is sanctuary for 44 Brothers (and, since 2018, some of the Brothers are women) at the almshouse at Charterhouse Square and thus right in the heart of London. What a fantastic address if you are able to move in. One of the pre-conditions for living there is that you have to be single; and while you are entitled to your own self-contained flat, the only obligation is to eat communally and be an active part of the community. You can tour the site and see the living quarters, chapel, library and garden.

Originally the land was a burial ground for Black Death victims. It then became a monastery for Carthusian monks (1371), who had their own cells, often with gardens and where conversation was restricted. After that, the history of Charterhouse changed and it probably became a noisy place; after the Dissolution, the site had a succession of private families living there. But after 1611 the sound level would have increased again, as it became a school for 44 poor boys and a hospital for 80 poor gentlemen.

It was founded by Thomas Sutton, whose body was later laid in the chapel beneath a beautifully carved tomb. So the building's status now is not such a far cry from its monastic origins and has remained as a place of special distinction and with this, a charitable status. Thomas More lived here for a while when he was a law student. Also, Thomas Cromwell (see ch. 21) came to visit the monks to tell them about Henry VIII's *Act of Supremacy*. The monks refused to recognise this and some were executed at Tyburn as a result.

Charterhouse Square has a particular feel about it: it is gated, although the gates are usually open. It is cobbled and the square is part residential. There is a commanding block of stunning 1930s flats and there are four-storey Georgian houses and scaffolding concealing even more building delights.

Address The Charterhouse, Charterhouse Square, EC1M 6AN, +44 (0)203 818 8873, www.thecharterhouse.org | Getting there Tube to Barbican (Circle, Hammersmith & City and Metropolitan Lines), Farringdon (Hammersmith & City Line); Crossrail to Farringdon; bus: 4, 56 or 153 | Hours Tue–Sat 11am–5.20pm | Tip The church is very close to St Bartholomew the Great and St Bartholomew the Less (see ch. 23) and the Barbican, an exciting arts venue in London.

20 Christchurch Greyfriars

How does your garden grow?

A ruined or partly destroyed church that has had to change its purpose is still a thing of value and quite often beauty. And you can still make out something of what it was, even with a changed purpose that often takes account of its original foundation. Like many City churches, the site has had a turbulent past: from monastery to site of destruction and in-between a school chapel. Its architecture was originally medieval, then Christopher Wren's design post the Great Fire and then a post Blitz deterioration. Finally, most of the church was destroyed when the General Post Office needed to expand.

The church once belonged to the Greyfriars Monastery, founded in 1225 by Franciscans, who wore grey habits. The place attracted the great and the good, such as the man who sought his fortune – Richard Whittington (c. 1354–1423), politician and merchant and who became London Mayor. He set up a library at the monastery with donations of books. This contributed to the existing collection of religious texts, which made the monastery a *stadium*, the medieval word that described a place of learning.

The church was also the location for the burials of illustrious kings and queens, but also those who sought to destabilise royal prerogative. For example, the Holy Maid of Kent, Elizabeth Barton, who preached against Henry VIII's second marriage, and in rather uncomfortable statements, prophesised that the king would die. So troublesome was she seen to be that she was hanged at Tyburn in 1534.

Now, do visit for the churchyard, where a very pretty garden has been created around the tower of the church. There is still enough of the building to give you a sense of its former scale and size. See if you can work out what form the shape of the garden takes. It is a lovely setting for a picnic in the summer and could not be closer to St Paul's Cathedral.

Address King Edward Street, EC1A 7BA, +44 (0)207 374 4127, www.cityoflondon.gov.uk |
Getting there Tube to St Paul's (Central Line, exit 2); bus: 3 or 74 | Hours Accessible
24 hours, exterior only | Tip The garden is situated very close to St Paul's Cathedral.

21___The Dutch Church

European London

Vincent van Gogh visited the Dutch church, possibly with his sister, to whom he gave a drawing of the building (1876). He wrote, 'this little church is a remarkable remnant of an old Augustinian foundation'. The church's founder (1250s, date varies) was Humphrey de Bohun, Constable of England. The Bohun family collected illuminated religious books that contained miniatures and illustrations of everyday people in them. Van Gogh is also famous as a vivid painter of the ordinary.

The church's address is 7 Austin Friars and thus an appropriate number, as there are many number 7s in Christian worship. The seven days of Creation, the seven virtues or vices and the seven days of the week. But there would have been more than seven friars resident here. In the 16th century, their neighbour was Thomas Cromwell (c. 1485–1540), adviser to Henry VIII, particularly in his marriage matters and who was instrumental in the beheading of Anne Boleyn. Cromwell is now a legendary figure, thanks to Hilary Mantel's novels. He had a large house next door from the 1520s and was directly involved in his religious neighbour being dissolved in 1538 during the Reformation. But then Cromwell was also himself dissolved in 1540 as the hushed corridors of Henry's houses became querulous and noisy, heralding the demise of the power hiatus that Cromwell had created for himself.

By 1550, the church had been given over to 'Germans and other strangers' who were able to use the church for their services. Downstairs is the Dutch Centre, a small museum that tells us that King Edward VI granted a charter to the Protestant refugees from the Low Countries in the former Augustinian church so that they had somewhere to worship. In its later history, we see how the church provided a conduit between the Protestants and immigrants. Austin Friars became a house of welcome for foreigners in a turbulent time.

Address 7 Austin Friars, EC2N 2HA, +44 (0)207 588 1684, www.dutchchurch.org.uk | **Getting there** Tube to Bank (Central, Waterloo & City and Northern Lines), Moorgate (Hammersmith & City Line); bus: 11, 21, 133 or 344 | **Hours** Mon noon–2pm, but best to check, and on Sun | **Tip** There are many other City churches to visit in the vicinity, including All Hallows-on-the-Wall and St Giles' Cripplegate (see ch. 27).

22 London Mithraeum

The ultra modern and the pagan

Before there were churches in London there were temples dedicated to pagan gods and goddesses and not just those famous Greek and Roman ones! Churches were often built on these ancient foundations and pinched some of the cults and practices, infusing them into the new religion. There is nowhere better to see this layering of history than at the London Mithraeum, a Roman temple (built 240CE) and absorbed by Bloomberg's European headquarters. Indeed, money is never very far away from a religious space, as funds were always needed to build and adorn to give it the requisite look. Water, too, was essential, for all religious places needed a source and supply for one ritual or another. Here the Walbrook River marks the Roman settlement.

This is an ultra-modern space though, as while the excavated temple below street level (discovered on a bomb site in 1952–54) has been given its own atmospheric enclosure, complete with a 'moody' audio installation, there is also an area dedicated to displays of contemporary art. This is an aesthetic fusion of tradition and innovation, where imaginative curating brings the old and the new together. Artefacts from the more recent site excavation (2012–14), including pottery, pewter, writing tablets and animals, have been found.

The actual temple ruin has the similar layout of a church, with a nave, south and north aisles, columns to separate the areas and an apse where on some sort of dais would have been a statue or figure of Mithras, the temple's dedicatee saint. Not much is known about Mithras, except that he killed a bull, which means he may have had associations with a creation myth to do with fertility. A reconstructed head shows him with short curly hair, elegant, contoured facial features and a face of youthful strength and vigour.

The ideal male beauty. So why wouldn't you want to go and pay him homage?

23 St Bartholomew the Less

An ancient foundation for curing and healing

This chapel space, less well-known than its greater counterpart of St Bartholomew the Great, is round the corner in the complex of St Bartholomew's Hospital. But that does not mean that less is less great than the great! The chapel may be lesser in size, and less well-known, but that does not make it any the less. Like Middlesex Hospital, this fits into hospital chapel territory and is a charming, refined space. And this hospital has credible medieval legacies – it was founded in 1148 for the hospital of St Bartholomew, and is purportedly the oldest hospital in London. The hospital's foundation reflects the religious exhortation to give as well as receive, and if you can find and purchase land, do something altruistic with it.

When Rahere (d. 1144) became ill with malaria while on pilgrimage, he decided to build a hospital and priory as thanks for his survival, and this is what he did. Luckily for him, Henry I bestowed him land just outside the city wall and the sick and infirm, the poor and even travellers could be cared for. Unlike a lot of religious institutions that became privately owned after the Reformation, when the priory was closed by Henry VIII, the hospital continued to function. So you might be surprised to see a monument to Henry over the gateway. Recognising perhaps that people needed somewhere to be sick, the king reopened the hospital in 1544.

The interior of the chapel is now 18th century, built under the architect George Dance the Younger (1741–1825). And it is said that relics, which the hospital owned of both the True Cross and Bartholomew, were used in the healing process.

There is a classicising monument to Queen Elizabeth I's surgeon, Robert Balthrope (d. 1591), who is shown in sculptural form kneeling on a cushion and with arms clasped tightly across his body. Even those in higher echelons of society need protection.

Tread carefully to reveal a rather fine brass rubbing.

Address 57a West Smithfield, EC1A 9DS, +44 (0)207 600 0440, www.greatstbarts.com/about/st-barts-the-less | Getting there Tube to Barbican (Circle, Hammersmith & City and Metropolitan Lines); bus: 4, 25, 56 or 388 | Hours Daily 8am–10pm | Tip Nearby is the church of St Bartholomew the Great, the chapel at Charterhouse and the Barbican Arts Centre.

24 St Botolph-Aldersgate

The patron saint of travelling

St Botolph is not the only church designated Botolph in London, or indeed in England. Botolph (d. 680CE) is not a well-known saint, yet there are many churches named after him. He became the patron saint of travellers in Anglo-Saxon times. Quite often his churches are situated near city gateways or entrances, or places that mark stages on a journey. The original church was built by Aldersgate, which had been constructed by the Romans. Samuel Pepys (1633–1703) saw the limbs of traitors hanging from the exterior, but it was demolished in 1761.

The building (its present construction dates back to 1788–91) is as much about the church as its leafy location, its beautiful white classical façade and its elegant brick tower rising into a white stone spire. It is also about encounters and conversations with others. When you go, you might be welcomed as a weary traveller with friendly hospitality by a man at a desk and another who might offer you a quick tour of the church. This is a very friendly place.

You will see a stunning 18th-century painting made to look like stained glass, which is easy to mistake for real stained glass. The subject matter is the *Agony in the Garden*, which took place after the Last Supper when Christ goes into the Garden of Gethsemane to pray with Peter, James and John. Here, though, Christ is alone except for two angels.

The church as a place to encourage prayer for the dead seems to be in the most appropriate setting, right beside Postman's Park. This was designed by the Victorian artist G. F. Watts (1817–1904) as a memorial to heroic civilian deaths. Here are beautifully made tiles, each recording quite often heartbreaking memorials to the dead, such as *William Fisher, aged 9, lost his life on Rodney Road, Walworth, while trying to save his little brother from being run over, July 12, 1886.*

Here at this lovely church, you can remember.

Address Aldersgate Street, EC1A 4EU, +44 (0)207 606 0684, www.stbotolphsaldersgate.org.uk | Getting there Tube to Barbican (Circle, Hammersmith & City and Metropolitan Lines), St Paul's (Central Line); bus: 25, 46 or 172 | Hours Tue 1pm to hear a short talk from the Bible, ending at 1.40pm | Tip Nearby is the Museum of London, with a wonderful collection of artefacts relating to the history of London (www.museumoflondon.org.uk).

25 — St Bride

Crypt museum and ancient walls

St Bride (451–525CE), founded a nunnery in 470CE in Kildare with a small group of nuns. It was a centre of illuminated manuscript production, in keeping with this church's later reputation as the centre for journalism and the printing industry. See the Bride cross over the north door – allegedly she made a cross out of rushes, which she gave to a dying man.

The name 'Bride' may also be appropriate as Christopher Wren's legendary spire (1701–3) is likened to a wedding cake, due to an 18th-century anecdote that a Mr Rich wanted a wedding cake to look like St Bride's spire with all its tiers. Much of the current church was rebuilt after World War II, although it had been rebuilt in 1674, giving the building its substantial classicising architecture, proportions and symmetry. Note the barrel-vaulted ceiling nave. There is the most beautiful mini dome at the west entrance, best viewed inside. Note too, arches with rounded pediments, revealing the emphasis on the circle in the church.

The church is tucked away in a little churchyard. Here Wynkyn de Worde set up England's first printing press with moveable type in 1501 (note the stone memorial to him inside on the west wall). Many journalists and editors are commemorated with their names on the pew seats. And at a small altar, you will see lots of small photographic memorials to people from journalism who have recently died. Another historical figure associated with the word and church is the famous diarist Samuel Pepys who was baptised here.

Visit two small chapels in the crypt museum, along with architectural fragments, Roman counters, bones, pottery, flagons, oyster shells and ancient walls. See the iron coffin, intended to be used for 'the safety of the dead', at a time of rampant body snatching. However, wooden coffins were deemed preferable, as they took less time to disintegrate.

Address Fleet Street, EC4Y 8AU, +44 (0)207 427 0133, www.stbrides.com/index.php | Getting there Mainline to Blackfriars (Thameslink); Tube to St Paul's (Central Line), Blackfriars (Circle and District Lines); bus: 4, 11, 15, 23, 26, 76 or 172 | Hours Mon–Fri 8am– 6pm, Sat 10am–3.30pm, Sun 10am–6.30pm | Tip Just 5 minutes' walk away is the charming house of Dr Johnson (www.drjohnsonshouse.org). Also St Bride Library, a wonderful collection of books about printing, typography and graphic design (www.sbf.org.uk/library).

26__St Dunstan in the East

An ivy-clad romantic ruin

This was once a church, dating back to 1100, but now it is a shell, apart from the tower, which was built by Sir Christopher Wren (1695–1701). This is a fairly remarkable thing, as nearly all of the City churches' towers were destroyed in the Great Fire (1666). But most of this church was then destroyed in the Blitz during World War II.

Still, it is a very lovely shell, a place to sit, a place to idle in, a place to dream, a place to forget. Enter from Idol Lane and see how the ivy grows on fragments of the building, and how arches are partly concealed by foliage. There are disjointed stones and trailing vegetation. Here at St Dunstan we are in a place for all reasons and all seasons, as whether there is green, or mist or snow, or even rain, the effect on the place in all weathers is simply magical.

What remains shows how the consequence of a tragic twist of fate turns into fortune. It is rather like a poetic ruin, redolent of ruined buildings that became so fashionable during the period known as Romanticism in the 19th century, where plants trailing around corners and piers of buildings were a common feature to celebrate the unintentional wonder of broken walls. Although 'firsts' in styles are often pre-dated by events that actually only later establish an aesthetic.

In 1740, one Lord Belvedere, in West Meath, built himself a ruined abbey, intentionally blocking his view from his brother's house, as his wife had allegedly been having an affair with the said brother. So, there was a conceit of building romantic ruins for a purpose, as well as allowing them to stay as ruins, as we see here.

St Dunstan (c. 910–88) was a legendary Canterbury man, a monk with a colourful past who became an archbishop. He is legendary for other reasons too: he was a scribe, a metalworker, an illuminator and even composed music. Multitasking is not just a modern phenomenon.

Address St Dunstan's Hill, EC3R 5DD, +44 (0)207 374 4127, www.cityoflondon.gov.uk/things-to-do/green-spaces | **Getting there** Tube to Monument or Tower Hill (District Line); bus: 15 or 40 | **Hours** Daily 8am–7pm, or dusk, whichever is earlier, closed Christmas Day, Boxing Day and New Year's Day | **Tip** A short walk up Eastcheap and then down Fish Street Hill will take you to the Monument to the Fire of London.

27 _ St Giles' Cripplegate
Homage to John Milton

St Giles church, now without the old Roman Cripplegate, is sunk in a sort of basin, both of water in the form of modern moat-like foundations and fountains, and the architecture of the Barbican. What was an ancient medieval church, is now surrounded by the brutal burst of modernity that is the Barbican's arts centre and apartments.

The church is dedicated to St Giles, the patron saint of indigents. He is also known as the patron saint of cripples, which you cannot help seeing in the name Cripplegate, though the word may have originally been 'cruplegate', meaning tunnel, and therefore has nothing to do with cripples. Above the north door is a niche carving of St Giles with his attribute, a hind. Legend has it that a king was out hunting and shot an arrow into a hind. Giles found the animal and healed it.

In the south aisle is a metal statue of John Milton (1608–74) author of *Paradise Lost* (1658–64), made by Horace Montford (c. 1840–1919). This is also Milton's burial site. The church is associated with William Shakespeare who worshipped at the church, having lodged in Silver Street, Cripplegate for a while and whose brother Edmund lived in the neighbourhood. Oliver Cromwell (1599–1658) of the Civil War, rather than the Tudor Cromwell, married Elizabeth Bouchier, a local girl, in the church in 1620. Thomas Stagg, whose gravestone is in the churchyard (d. 19 February, 1772), offers his own account of birth and death and life with the statement 'That is all'. Brevity is the soul of wit; brevity is the soul of Stagg.

John Foxe (1517–87), one of the church's preachers and also buried here, was the author of *Foxe's Book of Martyrs*, or *Actes and Monuments of these Latter and Perillous Days, Touching Matters of the Church, an account of Christian martyrs from the first century to the early 16th century*. This is his 'brief' account of the Protestant Martyrs!

Address Fore Street, EC2Y 8DA, +44 (0)207 638 1997, www.stgilesnewsite.co.uk |
Getting there Mainline to Moorgate (Great Northern); Tube to Moorgate (Circle,
Hammersmith & City, Metropolitan and Northern Lines), Barbican (Hammersmith
& City Line); bus: 8, 21, 25, 56, 76 or 100 | Hours Daily 9am – 6pm | Tip The church is
right beside the Barbican Arts Centre.

28 St James Garlickhythe

Not far from the wharf where garlic arrived

The church is dedicated to St James, the Great, whose relics are venerated by pilgrims all over the world at the cathedral of St James de Compostela in Spain. His attribute is the scallop shell and pictures of pilgrims show them with this motif on their travelling sacks. Inside the church you will see a scallop shell on top of the organ.

The church is called St James Garlickhythe, as the word *hythe* is an old Saxon word for 'landing stage', and it is thought that garlic from France, along with wine, was brought in by boats to a *hythe* nearby and then traded in Garlick Hill to the side of the church. It is no accident then that the church is located in the City ward of Vintry. London was a major port for foreign trade in the Middle Ages and other wharves in this part of London would have been the location for imports of silk and damask from the Middle East, woollen cloths from the Low Countries, wines from Europe and spices and dyestuffs from the East. And while it is generally assumed that garlic became widespread in this country under the pioneering influence of the cookery writer, Elizabeth David, who introduced post-war England to a Mediterranean diet, the trade in garlic suggests otherwise. The church is also situated just moments from the river.

Although the church, like most churches, has an Anglo-Saxon or later medieval origin, its present appearance dates back to Sir Christopher Wren's building of it (from 1676). The tower is complex and detailed and an excellent example of the architect's extraordinary visionary expertise. The church also lets in some wonderful natural light, as it seems Wren was also an alchemist enabling just the right quality of light in a building.

A bust of Thomas Cranmer (1489–1556) by Mary Quinn (1989) is found inside. She is a sculptor in bronze and has made many busts of famous people, such as St Teresa of Calcutta.

Address Garlick Hill, EC4V 2AF, +44 (0)7912 583 201, www.stjamesgarlickhythe.org |
Getting there Mainline to Cannon Street (Southeastern); Tube to Mansion House
(Circle and District Lines), Cannon Street (Circle and District Lines); bus: 15, 21 or 133 |
Hours Mon, Tue & Wed 8am–3pm, Thu 11am–3pm, Sun 7am–1pm | Tip Walk down
to the shore of the River Thames and go mudlarking (though you need a licence from
www.pla.co.uk/Environment/Thames-foreshore-permits). The church is not far from the
London Mithraeum (see ch. 22) or St Mary Aldermary (see ch. 32).

29_ St Katharine Cree

The next best thing to Renaissance Florence

St Katherine of Alexandria (d. 315CE?) refused a man for God. This man was the Roman Emperor Maxentius (c. 276–312CE), who thought he knew better and declared that she should be his wife; so put her to the test by challenging her to a debate with 50 philosophers. As she defeated them with her quick wit, the Emperor put the poor fellows to death. He then tried to torture her on the wheel (as in the Catherine Wheel of fireworks fame). But God prevailed with a comforting thunderbolt and she was saved, if but briefly. For she was then beheaded – hence her martyrdom status. You will see her depicted here in a stained glass window. Rather than the customary wheel, she is holding the martyr's palm, a lovely green frond. Katherine is also the same saint whose name begins with a 'C'. The C of Cree here is thought to have derived from Christchurch.

The Renaissance in London? The church's rebuilt interior consists of a colonnaded nave, reminiscent of many of the church designs of the great architect Filippo Brunelleschi (1377–1446), who built the Dome in Florence, as well as colonnaded churches as we see here.

Go inside and see classically inspired columns with acanthus leaf capitals rising into round headed arches. Unusually perhaps, they are painted blue and fraternise with the side aisles, which have blue-ribbed vaulting on them. So while the church looks similar to a Renaissance church, there are older, medieval features, although most of the body of the church we see today is 17th century. At the right of the altar is a rather dirty effigy – the quintessential knight likeness. He lies on crisply carved stone to act as a sort of bed sheet or shroud. He wears a bulbous skirt incised and impressed with the tools of the stone carver and above, a breast plate. It is hard to see his expression and he does not have a little dog or lion at his feet. Poor lonely knight. Then again, he is in a very elegant church.

THIS DO IN REMEMBRANCE OF ME

Address 86 Leadenhall Street, EC3A 3BP, +44 (0)207 488 4318 | Getting there Mainline to Fenchurch Street (c2c); Tube to Aldgate (Circle and Metropolitan Lines), Monument (Circle and District Lines); bus: 25 or 40 | Hours Tue 11am–3pm, Wed & Thu 1.05–2pm, Sun 1–3pm | Tip The church is close to the Gherkin and the Guildhall, where the Guildhall Art Gallery has a very good collection of Victorian art (www.guildhall.cityoflondon.gov.uk/art-gallery).

30 St Magnus the Martyr
An Orkney saint and a 20th-century poet

St Magnus came from Orkney and here in the City of London is a church (present building Sir Christopher Wren 1671–87) dedicated to him, showing us that saints (and even their well-travelled relics!) have the power to connect place, age and time.

Place here is important for other reasons: the church is situated as close as it gets to the River Thames and London Bridge and was at the centre of wharf and trading activity in the Middle Ages. In addition, in his legendary poem *The Wasteland*, T. S. Eliot refers to this church and the 'crowd' of people walking over London Bridge. And then place is another player with the big church clock that famously juts out over the bridge. It is thought to have been built following a vow by Sir Charles Duncombe (1648–1711) who once had to wait a long time in a cart on the bridge, without knowing the time. So there and then, he decided that if he ever could, he would give St Magnus a public clock. Although, like all good anecdotes, this is one of many that describe the foundation of the clock.

Poignantly for St Magnus, place plays a bad role too. Where is the 'inexplicable splendor of Ionian white and gold' shining as in Eliot's poem? While he may have been referring to the church's classical splendour, the church's location is truly now a wasteland: ugly buildings, a grim, grey, highway running beside the church causing a ceaseless throbbing of fume and pollution. The church's foundations must shake with every passing car. But now the east–west super cycle highway is there, and maybe as more go past by bicycle (or walking), it will become less grey, more clean and white and radiant if cars diminish.

While now the building seems so misaligned, as it clings to water and road, saved against the odds by various catastrophes such as fire and threats of closure, let's hope that the might of Eliot's words will keep it there.

Address Lower Thames Street, EC3R 6DN, +44 (0)207 626 4481, www.stmagnusmartyr.org.uk |
Getting there Mainline to Cannon Street (Southeastern); Tube to Cannon Street (Circle and
District Lines), Liverpool Street (Central, Circle, Hammersmith & City and Metropolitan
Lines); bus: 15, 47, 48, 141 or 344 | **Hours** Tue–Fri 10am–4pm | **Tip** See St Mary Woolnoth
(see ch. 33) too, the other church mentioned in *The Wasteland*. The church is very close to
St Dunstan in the East (see ch. 26) and London Bridge.

31 St Margaret Pattens

Pattens protect you from mud and rain

Enter at your peril if you ignore what the notice commands: *Will the women remove their pattens before entering the church and the men wipe their shoes on the mat.* This relates to the dedication of the church to the craft of patten making. Pattens were outdoor shoes with a wooden or metal sole, and an iron ring to elevate them, with a cloth or leather strap to protect your normal shoe. They were needed on the muddy and messy streets of London, especially for women who wore them to protect their long dresses from getting dirty. Jane Austen describes Lady Russell entering Bath in her pattens in *Persuasion* (1818).

This church was where the patten makers would worship, and now in the vestibule there is a little museum dedicated to this ancient craft, with display cases containing examples. Although the craft died out in the 19th century, when the pavements you now walk on became smooth, and clean and commodious, the Worshipful Company of Pattenmakers is still one of the 110 City of London Livery Companies. Yet, you might also wonder if it is a museum of basket making, for on the left in the vestibule of the church is a display case of baskets! This is not so odd, as the church became a guild church in 1954, which explains the celebration of the dual craft of basket and shoe making.

Inside, is a monument to Charles I (reign 1625–49), which refers to him as 'King and Martyr'. Every year, he is commemorated in a special service. The wooden pews and pulpit inside are a reminder of the fact that this church was originally a wooden chapel, founded in 1067 and dedicated to St Margaret of Antioch, a martyr saint, who was skilled at beating demons. The current church was designed by Sir Christopher Wren (from 1684) and, at the time, its spire would have stood out on the London skyline. Now, it is a little dwarfed by the skyscraper known as the 'Walkie Talkie'.

Address Rood Lane, Eastcheap, EC3M 1HS, +44 (0)20 7623 6630,
www.stmargaretpattens.org | Getting there Mainline to Fenchurch Street (c2c), Cannon
Street (Southeastern); Tube to Monument (Circle and District Lines), Bank (Central,
Circle, District, Northern and Waterloo & City Lines); bus: 15 | Hours Mon–Fri 8am–late
afternoon | Tip You can go up to the Sky Garden on the 43rd floor of the Walkie Talkie for
a drink and to admire the view (www.skygarden.london).

32__St Mary Aldermary
The three C words

These words are church, coffee and café. And I suspect the latter has cake, so that makes four. The church of St Mary Aldermary, from the Old English, 'older Mary', offers an unusual location to drink coffee in their appropriately named café, Host, in the elegant nave. The altar has been spared as the counter to serve the coffee, presumably because at times it is still used for the Eucharist ritual: for the distribution of wine and wafer. Go to the counter at the other end of the nave to order, then sit down and take in the space. Look up to see the fan vaulting above, which would tire you if you had to stand all the time. This was probably done by the celebrated plasterer Henry Doogood, possibly under the supervision of Christopher Wren. The current church was erected between 1679 and 1682; it is the only City church that was rebuilt in the Gothic style after the Great Fire of London (1666).

While the church is not always quiet, it is lovely to get a sense of coming together in the space. You can sit down and watch people talking and meditating (for that is encouraged here too). And if this jars, it shouldn't, as while we might think that apart from when a service is on, a church should be a silent place, we know that medieval churches were full of many varieties of people: scholars, monks, children, wives, mothers, grandmothers, young and old, even itinerants and beggars, and they would have all made quite a sound. The church's space is being brought back to life, even if it is through our daily need for that hearty brown liquid. Look up to one of the previously mentioned vaults. Imagine them opening to let in swooping angels and crows to dive and duck and take the crumbs from your bun or croissant.

This is a sensational place to have coffee, entered from a little courtyard with a tree growing in it. A tiny piece of Paradise in the City.

Address 69 Watling Street, EC4N 4SJ, +44 (0)207 248 9902, www.london-city-churches.org.uk/Churches/StMaryAldermary/index.html | **Getting there** Tube to Mansion House (Circle and District Lines), Bank (Central, Waterloo & City and Northern Lines); bus: 3, 15 or 115 | **Hours** Mon–Thu 7.30am–4.30pm, Fri to 4pm | **Tip** Not far away is the Church of St Mary le Bow, with a very good crypt café to continue coffee drinking in churches.

33 St Mary Woolnoth

T. S. Eliot's legendary poem The Waste Land

St Mary Woolnoth is one of the churches in the City of London made famous by T. S. Eliot's poem, *The Waste Land*. Walk away from the church along King William Street, and you can imagine passing the poet returning to 2020s London in his trilby. Would he be muttering about the noise, the grime, the crowds and the cold? Would he be wondering about the waste in the bright bags left at the street corners or comment on all the used-up land? Would he wish to rewrite his poem?

The name Woolnoth may be a derivation from one of the medieval benefactors, one Wulnoth de Walebrok. The deed of Wilnotmaricherche (not a spelling mistake!), dated to 1191, makes a connection to the founder of the church – a Saxon called Wulfnoth, built on the site of a Roman temple. The church was repaired by Sir Christopher Wren after the Great Fire of 1666 and rebuilt again by Sir Nicholas Hawksmoor (1716–27). William Butterfield took over works (1875–76) and he removed all the galleries.

The church is a reminder of just what dirt and dust can do to architectural fabric. Here, all is covered by grime at the edges and corners. There are three cherubs at the side of the church. They seem hardly immortal as youthfully cherubic and innocent things, but grey, abandoned and forgotten about. Indeed, with their blackened faces, they could almost be the City's climbing boys, eventually swept away by the philanthropy of late 19th-century kindly gentlemen, such as Lord Shaftesbury. And the cherubs are repeated neatly in a row above the altar inside the church, above large and curly lettering on boards, words from the *Book of Exodus*, The Ten Commandments and the Lord's Prayer. Luckily, they are a lot cleaner.

There is a powerful contemporary sculpture of the Madonna and Child by Jean Lamb, where Mary shows her adoration and reverence to the Christ child, as she leans her hand on her arms.

Address Lombard Street, EC3V 9EA, +44 (0)207 726 4878, www.stml.org.uk | Getting there DLR to Bank; Tube to Bank (exit 2, Central, Waterloo & City and Northern Lines), Mansion House (Circle and District Lines); bus: 8, 11, 21, 133 or 344 | Hours Mon–Fri 7.30am–5.15pm | Tip Many other City churches to visit and the church is very close to the Bank of England.

34 St Vedast-alias-Foster
A church with a cute sculpture garden at the back

St Vedast (d. c. 540CE) corrupted from the Norman St Vaast, is a little-known Frankish saint, who was the bishop of Arras. The Foster is also a derivation from Vedast. The church is on Foster Lane, just off Cheapside and close to St Paul's Cathedral. From its base, the tower, which you see from further away, rises to a blind arch above a doorway. There is a small roundel for a window, topped by a wider opening separated by a column, above which the glory of the twin towered bell turret gracefully inclines upwards. Here are balletic protrusions of corners, the rough stone edged by brick announcing and heralding the church's existence. It was probably designed by Robert Hooke (1690s), under Sir Christopher Wren.

The interior feels very different as it was refurnished after World War II damage, although that is hard to believe, as it feels rather like a medieval collegiate dining hall, containing little fabric lamp lights and shiny brown benches and pews. These actually obscure a rather majestic white rendered colonnade behind, on the south side. And at the apex of the arches, cherub heads are carved into roundels looking out at us – a striking contrast to the small icon of the Madonna and Child to the right of the high altar, angular and neatly painted. At the altar, the hue of purple drenching a velvet drape hangs down, glory mixing with the red hue of the red cushioned pews. You can also see the moving monument to a mother who died so young.

The small sculpture garden at the back is not to be missed. It has a tree in the middle and is framed by a red brick building and a small cloister to sit in. A Jacob Epstein bust head sits on a narrow ledge. There are also framed fragments of a Roman wall and a *putto* by the alarm system; his hand is either shielding himself from the noise with a cloth over his ear, or he is healing himself from a retaliating arrow.

Address 4 Foster Lane, EC2V 6HH, +44 (0)207 606 3998, www.vedast.org.uk | Getting there Tube to St Paul's (Central Line); bus: 3, 11, 17, 25, 43, 56, 76 or 133 | Hours Mon–Fri 8am–5.30pm, Sat 11am–4pm, Sun for service | Tip Two of many City churches you can visit in the vicinity include St Mary-le-Bow and St Paul's Cathedral.

35_Courland Grove Baptist

A perfectly proportioned house

How does one describe this perfect, perfectly proportioned gem of a building, with the name and date 1840 on the front? It is made of London brick with large windows, two either side of the doorway and one above, and the most elegant entrance, consisting of a white plastered post and lintel system, with columns topped by Ionic capitals. Part of its appeal is because it looks like an elegant London town house in a Georgian residential square. Maybe that is not such a strange notion, as the Baptists originally met in people's houses. There are many chapels, both in London and beyond, belonging to the Baptists who started to establish their churches from the middle of the 17th century.

The building seems to have survived against the odds. All around is social housing and the criss-cross of badly planned streets, although the beautiful Larkhall Park is nearby. But what might seem like an incongruous location for the building makes it all the more endearing. Although of course, Baptist chapels are more likely to be found in deprived parts of towns.

The 17th-century Baptists wanted to do things differently. They were just one of many groups acting with similar intentions: the Quakers, the Ranters, the Sabbatarians, the Seekers and the Diggers. Generally, these are groups known as dissenters (as in disagree). In essence, Baptists steered away from Protestantism in England, as they wanted to be free to worship as they saw fit. But that is not the end of the story; for like many religious establishments, from that original genesis, they split into different forms and types of Baptist churches and worship.

Unfortunately, the chapel is only open on a Sunday or for the occasional service. But it is still worth visiting for the architecture, its proportions and this little architectural delight in the middle of quite an urban maze.

GROVE BAPTIST

Address Courland Grove, SW8 2PX, +44 (0)207 498 9870, www.findachurch.co.uk/
church/clapham-greater-london/26933.htm | Getting there Mainline to Wandsworth
(South Western); Tube to Stockwell (Victoria Line); bus: 77, 87 or P5 | Hours Accessible
24 hours | Tip For another lovely Baptist chapel, but in a very different area of London,
visit the Bethseda Baptist chapel in Kensington Place.

36 Holy Trinity
Abolishing slavery

The rectangular brick church stands proud and elegant on Clapham Common. The current church dates to 1776 and replaces a much older church, as is the case with many London churches. The architect was Kenton Couse (1721–90) who also designed the front and steps of 10 Downing Street. Old engravings of the church show people going by in horse and carts, riders on horses all conveying an air of gentility. The church's size owes something to the fact that the growing congregation lived in rather elegant and large houses on Clapham Common, which you can still see today. The church was badly bombed in World War II, but you still get a sense of its 18th-century refinement with its large and bold architectural features.

One of the founding supporters of the church was John Thornton (1720–90), a rich merchant and banker, who had been involved in the new church foundation and Henry Venn, the Rector, who wrote a theological treatise called *The Complete Duty of Man* (1763).

The church was the location as a place of worship for members of an important sect dedicated to the abolition of slavery. The sect consisted of a group of men including William Wilberforce (1759–1833) who set up the organisation in 1780. Wilberforce made his first speech about it in the House of Commons in 1789. Another member was Henry Thornton, son of John (1760–1815), and great grandfather to the novelist E. M. Forster (1879–1970), author of novels such as *A Room with a View*, who was also baptised in the church. The sect also stressed the value of doing good coupled with seriousness and domestic religious observance. They also set out to promote humanitarian causes, especially ending slavery. You will see a blue plaque dedicated to the sect outside the church. Eventually, Parliament passed the act that made slave trading illegal in 1807, although it took longer than that to fully implement beyond the legislation.

Address Clapham Common Northside, SW4 OQZ, +44 (0)207 627 0941,
www.holytrinityclapham.org | Getting there Overground to Clapham High Street; Tube to
Clapham Common (Northern Line); bus: 37, 137, 155 or 345 | Hours Sun and Wed before
and after services; check website | Tip The church is on Clapham Common, so a lovely spot
to walk, or have a picnic right in front of the church.

37_St James

A church for designers

From a medieval Benedictine nunnery to now, a church that has the word 'Inspire' in its publicity, the dedicatee saint here is St James the Less, rather than James of Santiago de Compostela fame (see ch. 28 & 66). The Less was the son of Mary, the sister of the Virgin Mary and the brother of Jude who, like his brother, became an apostle. Accordingly, James never shaved, cut his hair, slept with women, drank wine, used a bath or oil, never wore sandals, and covered himself with one simple, linen garment. Despite being such a good boy, he was stoned to death. There is a statue of him made in wood over the west door to the nave.

St James is still a practising church, with a long and rich history. It is host to the annual designer fair situated right in the heart of Clerkenwell. This is a church that likes to be seen at the cutting edge of culture. That sense of performance continues as there are regular Wednesday lunchtime talks.

The church's origins go back to the Middle Ages. As it stands today, the church has 18th-century glimpses from the 1788–92 design by James Carr, a local architect, although it was restored by Sir Arthur Blomfield (1829–89) in 1882. He designed numerous churches and schools. A sturdy, but elegant tower rises into a tall steeple from the church foundation, with a wide span, articulated by a pedimented frontage. All is rational and proportional. The whole church is elevated, and so feels elegant in a setting of small streets. Yet you can still get a sense of how hierarchical the church used to be. For the upper galleries were designated for the poor, although the area was known for its philanthropy and charitable work too. Inside are the old benefaction boards, listing the charities in the Clerkenwell neighbourhood. And in the 19th century, it was a church right at the heart of radical thought and activity; after all, the Marx Memorial Library is just down the road.

Address Clerkenwell Close, EC1R 0EA, +44 (0)207 629 0874, www.inspiresaintjames.org | Getting there Mainline to Farringdon (Thameslink); Tube or Crossrail to Farringdon (Hammersmith & City and Metropolitan Lines); bus: 38, 55, 63 or 243 | Hours Mon–Fri 9am–6pm, Sun for service times | Tip Wander around Clerkenwell with its narrow streets, old warehouses and design studios.

38__St Peter

The altar in the west is close to the deli

A church built for 2,000 Italian immigrants in the area known as the Saffron Hill slums. The church dates to 1863, when Italians were working in the vicinity as musicians, organ grinders and artisans. It was built at a time when there was quite a lot of hostility to the Catholic faith.

The building is modelled on a Roman basilica and has a classical exterior. It is better to view the building from the opposite side of the road, as it is situated on quite a narrow pavement. You will then be in a good position to observe the loggia framed by two round headed arches, from which you enter the church. Above are two mosaics, one of which is of Jesus giving the keys to the Kingdom of Heaven to St Peter. Inside is a large space, with ornate side chapels and statues. You will know what I mean when I say it feels rather Italian! It is a joyous confection of colours and curls. You will also note that the altar is located at the west end of the church. Traditionally, churches have a west–east orientation, so that the high altar, the place for the priest to enact the most important liturgical ritual, Eucharist, is situated close to Jerusalem and at the church's east end. Here, though, the altar, while it faces east is situated to the left as you come in from the south.

It might be worth trying to visit the church when the bells are rung. It houses a very large bell indeed and, apart from Big Ben, is thought to be one of the largest bells in London – and presumably one of the loudest?

The church has had a dramatic history. In the entrance loggia is a memorial to some 446 Italians who lost their lives in the SS *Arandona Star*. This large liner transported Italian and German civilians and a small group of prisoners of war during World War II to Canada. However, on 2 July, 1940 the ship was sunk by a German U-boat, off the north-west coast of the United Kingdom.

Address 136 Clerkenwell Road, EC1R 5EN, +44 (0)207 837 1528, www.italianchurch.org.uk |
Getting there Mainline to Farringdon (Thameslink); Tube to Farringdon (Hammersmith
& City Line), Chancery Lane (Central Line), Barbican (Circle, Hammersmith & City and
Metropolitan Lines); bus: 38, 40, 55, 63 or 243 | **Hours** Mon–Sat 9am–4pm, last Sun of each
month 9am–2pm | **Tip** Next door is an Italian deli where you can have coffee. The church is
only about 10 minutes' walk from a museum dedicated to the Order of St John, at St John's
Gate (museumstjohn.org.uk).

39___St Constantine and St Helen

All that glitters and all that gold

Crystal Palace Park was much beloved by the 19th-century art critic John Ruskin, who walked up and down the hills of south-east London. Easy to miss and less well-known is the church of St Constantine and St Helen on a nondescript through road. Here is an interior of glittering gold, with painted angels on columns and holy figures on cupboards and walls. After the gloom of a grey street, the senses awaken, and it is hard to believe that you are in suburban London. The exterior is Victorian: there is a tower and a pointed arch framing the doorway, which is surmounted by a gable broken up by tracery to articulate the window. What a contrast to the quintessentially Greek Orthodox interior, where the altar, true to tradition, is located behind a wooden gate, and only opened when the priest officiates at services.

Sometimes, mothers and sons have good working relationships, as witnessed in this church. It is dedicated to Roman Emperor Constantine (ruled c. 272–337CE) and his mother, Helen (c. 248–330CE). She was good at finding things; for example, the True Cross, when she travelled to Palestine in 326–8CE, triggering the foundation of the church of the Holy Sepulchre in Jerusalem. Constantine had formally established Christianity in 312CE, making her find even more worthwhile. Many icons in the church depict him and his mother, but it is considered sacrilegious to stare at them for too long. The relics of a bishop who had attended the important Council of Nicaea in 325CE are also on show. The Council was a massive assembly of bishops and priests to represent Christendom where matters such as the date for Easter were set. History and religion here are profoundly intertwined. This is a place to go, to be, to stare and wonder without the filter of a phone. The church is full of sacred images, giving the space a spiritual majesty.

Address 69A Westow Street, SE19 3RW, +44 (0)208 653 6824, www.thyateira.org.uk/ the-greek-orthodox-church-of-ss-constantine-and-helen | Getting there Mainline to Gipsy Hill (Southern), Crystal Palace (Southern); Overground to Crystal Palace; bus: 249, 322, 417, 432 or 450 | Hours Any reasonable time, but best not to visit on Sunday mornings during services | Tip Visit the Crystal Palace junk and vintage shops for small models of the Virgin and Child.

40_St Saviour
Beautiful brutality

This magnificent church built on one of Henry VIII's hunting grounds, is on the 'Buildings at Risk Register'; so go before it is too late. Completed in 1933, it is a brutal but striking edifice, with staggeringly good architecture, even though the architect, N. F. (Nugent) Cachemaille-Day (1896–1976) put drainpipes inside the interior pillars, which has caused many a damp problem. But this means that the exterior's surfaces are clean and pristine; though design is not the only consideration when building a church. Still, you cannot really blame the architect, as he designed about 60 ravishingly revolutionary churches. His architecture puts the 20th century on the map. The building here is made up of encased concrete with brick, creating pure and simple lines and it really works. Does the exterior speak church, or does it speak prison?

Note the nave without aisles, but with two narrow passages running up north and south as a horizontal line to parallel the strong verticals of the brick piers. Perhaps, unexpectedly for such a modern building, there is a Lady Chapel with stunning abstract stained glass. Forgive the hyperbole, but this church was designed to astound.

The funding for St Saviour's came from the *25 Churches in Southwark Fund*, to coincide with the building of 2,000 houses in the neighbourhood for an estate under Woolwich Borough Council. At the south aisle is a cross on one of the piers; one of the distinctive wooden crosses to identify the 25 Southwark churches.

Look at one of the biggest statues that you will see anywhere of Christ holding an orb, while blessing with his other hand, in dense dark stone. What a contrast to the barren brick simplicity of the exterior. The statue's boldness is sustained in the stained glass behind Christ at the east end. Here are four tall vertical shaped windows (executed by Donald Hastings), slits all in blue: a celestial sky for the church goers.

Address Middle Park Avenue, Eltham, SE9 5JH, +44 (0)208 850 6829 | **Getting there** Mainline to Mottingham (Southeastern); bus: 124 or 161 | **Hours** Wed 9.30am for service, or by arrangement | **Tip** A 13-minute walk away is Eltham Palace, once a Tudor royal residence and now part Art Deco mansion (www.english-heritage.org.uk).

41 St Clement

Classical in a gorgeous green square

The church is situated on a square, with lots of trees and a green space opposite, where you can sit and admire the elegant building that is St Clement's. The square is surrounded by social housing, giving you an insight into the fascinating way in which London's architectural fabric and the different types of buildings grow in accordance with one another. This sort of juxtaposition also helps us to reimagine the past, as this area used to be open grazing land. In Shakespeare's *Henry IV* (Part One, Act III, Scene I), Hotspur says, 'as if thou never walk'st further than Finsbury'. And still you can walk there to see a lot of building development, but which has not diminished an older heritage.

The church has a classical temple front of real grandeur. Not so classical is the spire, looking very Gothic indeed. So timeless is the classical style, that with a bit of additional architectural miscellany, the style will not let the aesthetic requirement down. The architect was Philip Hardwick (1792–1870), who designed Euston Station entrance and the famous Euston Arch (demolished), which looked wholly like an ancient Roman triumphal arch. The church opened in 1824, the same year that the National Gallery (also with a large pedimented classical front) opened. Despite being bombed in World War II, the interior of the church has retained its grandiose classical feel.

There is often lovely terminology for different types of churches; here this church, originally assigned to St Barnabas, was a chapel of ease, an extra place of worship for those too far from their own parish church. But its size is really on a scale to emulate the Sistine chapel, not a small chapel. Then it became known as a Waterloo church as thanks for fighting and winning Napoleon. And the government then put aside £1 million for building churches where there were large populations.

Address King Square, EC1V 8DA, +44 (0)207 251 0706, www.stclementfinsbury.org | Getting there Tube to Angel (Northern Line), Old Street (Northern Line), Barbican (Circle, Hammersmith & City and Metropolitan Lines); bus: 4, 43, 55, 56, 205, 214 or 243 | Hours Daily 9am–5pm. Ask at the office next door to open church | Tip The church is located close to Shoreditch, an interesting area of London, full of cafés and bars.

42___St Alfege

Martyr saint and medieval nails

This church stands like a beacon of strength and vigour in the heart of Greenwich. It is situated as if on its own little island, and in its all white glamour looks ready to go to the ball. For this is an edifice of high-impact drama, with gigantic architecture: the portal, the pediment, the columns and the windows. Inside, though, the colours change and there is a wealth of wood, some carved by Grinling Gibbons (1648–1721), which gives the interior a quality that is warm and inviting, so that despite its size, the church feels cosy. The church might also be pleasing on the eye, as the architect was Nicholas Hawksmoor (1661–1736), who was working here from 1712–14. And as with many of his churches, the light seems right, the balance, the proportions and the symmetry are just enough to give a little bit of theatre and eloquence with imposing openings and galleries, but not without distracting from the altar as the main event.

St Alfege is also an interesting saint, as he was killed in 1012 by the Danes. But he was also Archbishop of Canterbury and not being satisfied with just doing away with him, the marauders burned his cathedral and thereafter for some reason took him to Greenwich and tried to ransom him. This is often the best way to make a martyr of somebody in Christianity, and of course this is exactly what happened.

The church has a charming plaque dedicated to a master musician of the Tudor and Elizabethan periods, one Thomas Tallis (1505–85), who worked for illustrious patrons such as Elizabeth I and Henry VIII and who was baptised and buried here. Among many highlights are the nails from the medieval Coventry Cross now on a table, and a moving reminder of the World War II bomb that hit Coventry Cathedral. At the time, they were probably nothing special, but in a different time and location have become like a sacred object.

Address Greenwich Church Street, SE10 9BJ, +44 (0)208 853 0687, www.st-alfege.org | Getting there Mainline to Greenwich (Southeastern); DLR to Greenwich or Cutty Sark; bus: 177, 180, 188, 199 or 386 | Hours Mon–Fri 11am–4pm, Sat 10am–4pm, Sun noon–4pm | Tip So much on offer nearby: the Queen's House, National Maritime Museum, Royal Naval College and the *Cutty Sark*.

43__St John
A concert venue

A large, inviting space, both in and out. The churchyard is a place to wander in and has paths all around it that are inviting for little ones. There is also a children's playground by the commanding church and steeple that rises way above the lively beings who jump and shout, cry and laugh, swing and run. The exterior space has multifunctional use: as a passageway from Clapton to Hackney, and then there is a medicinal garden and café, and of course the church itself.

The church was designed by James Spiller (1792–97). An elegant pedimented brick façade rises into a tower, standing proudly on the skyline. There is a large interior in the Greek cross plan. So, all four arms of the church are equal, the intention being that the altar should be in the middle of the church, so that the priest officiating would represent God at the four corners of the world as it were. Although quite often the Greek plan was compromised, as more space was required, and here an additional wall on one side of the church was added in the 19th century. In the case of this church that does seem striking, as it was originally designed to house 4,000 people. There is an earlier structure, from an earlier church – this is the 16th-century tower, all that is left of the building that was demolished to make way for the new.

The church has the most wonderful promotional video, illustrating the importance of a church's life in communities today. It also does a lot of outreach work and it thrives as the setting for bands and concerts; it has hosted singers like Ed Sheeran and bands like Coldplay.

There are some wonderful old tombs in the churchyard, including that of Joachim Conrad Loddiges (1738–1826). He was the founder of a nursery garden in Hackney, specialising in importing exotic plants. See if you can find a red door in the churchyard, identified as well by an inscription next to it.

Address Lower Clapton Road, Hackney, E5 0PD, +44 (0)208 986 2241,
www.hackney.church | Getting there Overground to Hackney Central; bus: 21 | Hours
Mon–Fri 9.30am–5.30pm | Tip The church is situated very close to a beautiful Tudor
National Trust property called Sutton House (www.nationaltrust.org.uk/sutton-house-
and-breakers-yard).

44_ St Michael & All Angels
Stunning murals

This modern church contains a cycle of murals (1961) that seem to be inspired by a rainbow palette, set against calf-yellow backgrounds. These were executed by John Hayward (1929–2007), principally known as a stained glass artist. The murals are bewitching. With limpid colours mirroring the best of Italian fresco cycles, bold figures are straight and majestic, and the narratives are easy to read. The *marouflage* technique was used, whereby the images are painted in the studio, then transferred and glued to the wall of the church.

The scenes on the north and south walls of the church include scenes from the Old and the New Testament. The *Baptism of Christ* is an unusual composition. John the Baptist's ritual of pouring water over Christ's head is seemingly symbolic rather than actual, as he holds up, as if to the light, a scallop shell, the symbol of pilgrimage. Also, John looks to his right, while Christ looks directly out at the spectator, and a dove, framed by a blood orange red surround, floats above him. John the Baptist's left foot is in the water, while his right foot is on dry ground. Christ's feet are not visible as they are submerged by the water of the River Jordan.

The figures of Adam and Eve are clothed in lots of green leaves, rather than just the one fig leaf covering up their genders. They could almost be green man neophytes. Their limbs, long and gangling and bent at the knees seem soft in response to the angular, Cubist measured form of the angel banishing them with his massive wingspan and flaming sword or staff. He seems to be at once angel and eagle.

Likewise, in the *Annunciation*, the angel Gabriel, though cloaked in white and overlain with a huge white wing, is strong, majestic, even ferocious. This is one of the most striking things about this cycle of paintings: the angels are more than mere messengers and have a real presence.

Address Lansdowne Drive, Hackney, E8 3ER, +44 (0)207 249 2627,
www.stmichaelslondonfields.org.uk | Getting there Overground to London Fields or
Hackney Central; bus: 38 | Hours Wed 9am–3pm, except between Christmas and New
Year and during the week after Easter | Tip London Fields is lovely for a stroll or a picnic
in the summer.

45__St Augustine
A superb architect redesign

St Augustine's restores your faith in humanity. Once a drab late-Victorian structure, a recent restoration by Roz Barr Architects radiates in fabric, textures, surfaces, materials, setting and light. A fitting tribute to the founding of the Augustinian order in 1244 in Tuscany where beautiful, clean and sharp light is found. With a modern, even Nordic twist, the space allows for either song or chat, noise or silence. And here is an active, open-all-day Catholic church with a treasure house of materials: oiled rafters brushed white; Venetian plaster of bulk and weight, hewn to make a sturdy altar on which are inscribed gold crosses; a tabernacle redolent of a futuristic space pod made out of cast iron; a carved wooden door to access the 'host', and a clean-lined oak lectern. Every available surface is tactile.

Look too at the hollowed disc elevated over the altar, like a fine strip of halo found on painted saints and Virgins in Renaissance painting. The Augustinian motto, *Veritas, Unitas, Caritas*, is discreetly written into the interior rim. It is simple, but contemporary, and a celebration of substance in a space dedicated to the spiritual. But this emphasis on touch is not out of place, as there is no denying that Christianity has always been a material culture that endorses the use of the rich wealth of materials to help us transcend our ordinary, everyday lives. And St Augustine himself was, before he became a monk, a somewhat hedonistic man who enjoyed the flesh! The church resonates with the philosophy of the great 19th-century artistic visionaries – William Morris and John Ruskin, which advocated the plain and simple at a time when the machine was taking precedence.

Even on a dark day, the church space exudes the best of the light. The church is the centre for the Austin Forum, which showcases art to encourage their mission of promoting spirituality.

Address 55 Fulham Palace Road, W6 8AU, +44 (0)208 748 3788, www.saintaugustineshammersmith.org | **Getting there** Tube to Hammersmith (District, Hammersmith & City and Piccadilly Lines); bus: 111, 220 or 237 | **Hours** Daily 9am–5pm and at service times | **Tip** While in this area, you can also visit Fulham Palace and Fulham Palace Chapel.

46_ St Mary

Standing still in the face of Heathrow expansion

A model of the tenacity of church buildings to survive against rapid change. While this ancient parish church might be saved if Heathrow airport expands, the community it serves will not. Harmondsworth is right in the middle of the proposed new flight path, and if that goes ahead, all the buildings in the immediate vicinity, except the church will be demolished.

The church and its village location is so quaint and cute, you can transport yourself back to the Middle Ages. Consider how the church and village were connected to other village locations, such as Hillingdon and West Drayton, and where once were waggons and horses, mules and people travelling. Here we see something of the ancient church building materials first used: timber and wattle construction and then tiled. Then there are the brown coloured materials blending in with the green and wheat colours of the fields that would have originally surrounded the church.

Effective communication channels existed even in the Middle Ages. The manor at the village was granted to William of Wykeham, Bishop of Winchester in 1389. And revenue went towards the maintenance of Winchester College in a medieval town called Winchester! Quite a long way away, but proof that travel links were not insurmountable.

Nikolaus Pevsner, the architectural historian, refers to the church doorway as being the most elaborate piece of Norman decoration in the country. See the zigzags, rosettes, *voussoirs* and squares.

There is a fascinating burial record for the church (1679). On 23 January, a woman called Susanna, referred to as a wandering person, was buried, *Without a local habitation, her wandering life, probably attended with many hardships and privations, terminated here in mid-winter.* The church's community might follow suit, so go and see this exotic structure before you take a flight elsewhere.

Address High Street, UB7 OAQ, 020 +44 (0)208 897 2385, www.stmarysharmondsworth.com | Getting there Mainline to West Drayton (Great Western Railway); Tube to Heathrow (Piccadilly Line, terminal 5), Heathrow Express (from Paddington); bus: 81, 350 or U3 | Hours Any suitable time with an appointment or on Sun before or after a service | Tip Next door is a stunning medieval tithe barn, another remnant of Harmondsworth's medieval past.

47 Our Lady of the Rosary
A little bit of Gothic France

Tusker Street in Kentish Town brings you to a path. There are two sections to the path, the first part interrupted by steps down to the second. On the right are the bays of what appears to be a very large church. This is one approach to the church of St Dominic's Priory, designed by John Chessell Buckler (1874–83) and which established itself as a self-serving religious community with a refectory and cloisters. Entering is like stepping into a small Gothic cathedral or at least an Italian basilica from the Middle Ages. The scale and size seem infinite, more surprising given this rather unattractive street in north London. This is an active, thriving church and one that has retained its sense of being a Gothic/medieval/Catholic church, even though the architectural fabric and design is essentially 19th century.

The interior is distinctive for its side chapels: at each space (and there are 14 of them, each dedicated to a mystery of the Rosary) is a carving of some aspect of religious belief such as the *Resurrection* or the *Road to Calvary*.

Even in a church off the radar of any tourist map, there is something of interest. Here, just sitting in a corner to the right as you enter, is an old column from an old Dominican church in Blackfriars – a column with a previous supporting or structural role, who knows?

As you would expect in a Catholic church, there are many statues. For example, the clasping, embracing image of the *Visitation*, when Elizabeth (John the Baptist's mother) and Mary greet one another to share in the joy that they will both give birth. The narrative is taken from *Luke* (1: 36–56) and is quite a common one told in Italian medieval and Renaissance fresco cycles. Here, one woman is standing, while the other is kneeling, providing a contrast in the figure arrangement. The way to tell who Mary is, is to look for a younger looking woman.

Address Southampton Road, NW5 4LB, +44 (0)207 482 9234, www.rosaryshrine.co.uk | Getting there Overground to Kentish Town West or Gospel Oak; Tube to Belsize Park (Northern Line); bus: 46 or C11 | Hours Daily 7.30am–6pm | Tip The church is just a 7-minute walk from the southern end of Hampstead Heath.

48 St Augustine of Canterbury

Sleeping Joseph

The church is situated at the top of a hill between Highgate and Archway near the big Archway bridge, where red buses thunder by.

The building is constructed of polychromed London masonry, and has an imposing central tower, with short abutments and buttresses attached. John Dando Sedding (1838–91) was the architect (see ch. 86) but he died prematurely so the building design was taken on by Henry Wilson (1864–1934). By 1910, the building, still not yet finished, required another architect, so after a competition to complete the west end (it is tradition to design the east end first), the job was given to J. Harold Gibbons (1878–1958).

The west end portal has a wide pointed arch and relief sculptures of the *Crucifixion* with Mary and John, beside the habitual figures at Crucifixion scenes. They are constructed in extensively carved and grooved drapery, very much in the idiom of Gothic sculpture, and reminiscent of statuary found on the great northern French cathedrals. Below, within the arch, is a statue of the Virgin and Child. Beneath the main sculptural group you will see a sleeping figure, resting his head in his left hand. This is Joseph shown as an old man to make this look like a *Nativity* scene. In this commonly depicted narrative, he is often shown asleep, having worked as hard as he did to bring his child Jesus into the world. This was made by one member of the Rope family, consisting of five daughters. Margaret Aldrich Rope (1891–1988), who trained at the Chelsea School of Art, did some stained glass in the church.

A tunnel vault runs down to the high altar. Throughout, there are passages of colour whether on ledges for painted sculptures, or altar frontals, hanging banners, gilded crosses on altars and stained glass.

Address Archway Road, N6 5BH, +44 (0)208 341 2564, www.saintaugustine.org.uk |
Getting there Overground to Crouch Hill; Tube to Highgate (Northern Line); bus: 32, 35,
39 or 53 | Hours Daily 8.30am–6pm | Tip The church is located 12 minutes' walk from
Highgate Village, which is a charming place to wander, and from there you can also visit
Highgate Cemetery.

49__Lincoln's Inn Chapel

The inner sanctum of the Inns of Court

Approach this chapel from Lincoln's Inn Fields, one of many largely unspoilt garden squares. Enter the grandiose portal to the Inns of Court and go into New Court (which really looks lovely and old). Follow the signs to 'Old Buildings' and all around see courtyards and passages and wide open, tree-lined paths. Then you will come to the wide span of perpendicular vaulting, which is the undercroft to the chapel. You then walk up a stone staircase, pass the boot scraper and see a brown door (usually closed). Open this door and, to the right of this hallway, is another brown door, which you open to take you into the chapel (dating from 1620–23, Inigo Jones). This is the chapel for the Lincoln's Inn Society of Barristers.

The interior contains many pews, presumably for the many barristers who would have worshipped here. There are three colourful stained glass windows of Apostles, and *Old Testament* figures with coats of arms to important people connected to the Inns below. And then at the window above the high altar and one to each side are many panels dedicated to the Treasurers of the Inn, including one for John George Butcher, Baron Danesfort, Treasurer (1926). But you will note that for him, instead of a coat of arms, there is an elephant. The angels in the chapel also testify to the role of the legal profession here – they are carved onto corbels and also hold coats of arms. Not far from this is a tiny alabaster fragment dating to the 14th century, which was originally part of a carved altar. You can just make out some of the colouring on it, as most sculptures were painted once they had been carved.

In the vestibule where you come in, is an inscription in Latin to Spencer Perceval (see ch. 16) and a portrait of the Metaphysical poet John Donne (1572–1631), who was a student at Lincoln's Inn, and who wrote one of his poems, *The Good Morrow*, during this time.

Address Treasury House, Lincoln's Inn, WC2A 3TL, +44 (0)207 405 1393, www.lincolnsinn.org.uk/about-us/chapel | **Getting there** Mainline to Charing Cross (Southeastern), Blackfriars (Thameslink); Tube to Blackfriars (Circle and District Lines), Temple (Circle and District Lines), Chancery Lane (Central Line); bus: 1, 15, 55, 168, 171 or 188 | **Hours** Mon–Fri 9am–5pm, Sun in term (check website) | **Tip** At the north end of Lincoln's Inn Fields is the Sir John Soane Museum, the house that belonged to the architect of the Bank of England (www.soane.org).

50__St Alban the Martyr

At the end of a little labyrinth of paths

This church was originally built by the Gothic Revivalist architect William Butterfield (1814–1900) and consecrated in 1863. Like so many churches in London, the building was built around real poverty and squalor. The expense and labour that went into building Victorian churches was partly done, it was thought, to alleviate the hardship that the local congregation were experiencing, in a sense to lift them spiritually from their misery. And the Victorian fabrics and furnishings and decoration played a role. While they might still retain an air of that period, most of the church was rebuilt after bomb damage in World War II.

The best time to visit this church is at dusk, as the light then is very beautiful. You walk through a passageway and an alleyway (beware, it can feel a bit sepulchral), turn a corner, then pass through the entrance to another courtyard that takes you to the church door. On the way, you will just make out some burial fragments.

After the noise of the Gray's Inn Road, the utter silence is a surprise. All the more so because, at this time, the church is only lit by two lights at the back, that is to say at the west end. You can sit down and look all the way down to the high altar (this is a long church), cloaked in darkness. And once your eyes have adjusted to the light, you can just make out various colours on images.

On the north side of the nave is a tract attached to the wall (very much in the spirit of Tractarianism) urging people not to accept the overnight transformation of one religion for another in the Reformation period. It was written along the lines of 'Don't believe a word of what you hear about the Reformation'. It gives you a sense that things are never as clear-cut as they seem with significant historical events. On the east wall is a striking Hans Feibusch mural of the *Resurrection*. Note the variety of gestures from the witnesses to the event.

Address 18 Brooke Street, EC1N 7RD, +44 (0)0207 430 2551, www.stalbansholborn.co.uk |
Getting there Mainline to Farringdon (Thameslink); Tube to Chancery Lane (Central Line,
exit 2), Farringdon (Hammersmith & City Line); Crossrail to Farringdon; bus: 8, 9, 17, 24,
25, 38, 45, 46, 242 or 521 | Hours Mon–Fri 8am–6pm | Tip On the corner of Brooke Street
and Gray's Inn Road there is the wonderful Konditor & Cook bakery/café.

51 St Etheldreda

Built by the abbess Etheldreda in the 7th century

Walk down Ely Place, with its iron gates, and at the end is this lovely church. Imagine being here when this was a large medieval palace for the bishops of Ely. The church then became a private chapel of William de Luda, Bishop of Ely, effectively a branch establishment attached to the Fenland town of Ely. It is thought that Henry VIII first met Thomas Cranmer (1489–1556), architect of the Reformation here. And in about 1620, Roman Catholics could worship at the church in secret, as the Spanish Ambassador was living in Ely Place. The uncle of Sir Christopher Wren, Matthew Wren (1585–1667) practised here as Bishop of Ely, but since it was deemed his services were too Catholic, he was imprisoned at the Tower (1642–60). The Rosminians (founded by Antonio Rosmini c. 1828), were based here from 1874; a religious charitable group who cared for the large Irish immigrant population in the area.

St Etheldreda (630–79CE) married twice: first to Tondbert, a prince (in virginal state) and then Egfrith, the king of Northumbria, in continuing virginal state, although she then decided that her vocation was religious. She was not only the founder of Ely Cathedral, but of the double monastery there (673CE).

One of the most charming things about the church is that it is on two storeys. This was common in the 13th century. The crypt, the lower part, is a beautiful atmospheric space, and where people took shelter during bombing raids in 1940. The upper church is a stunning Gothic arched space, full of intricate traceries. On the walls of the church are some statues of those who refused to support Henry VIII in having his first marriage annulled. The west window (1964) depicts the martyrdom in 1535 of three Catholic priests at Tyburn, including one who had been based at Charterhouse (see ch. 19) called John Houghton (1486–1535). Here, too, is St Etheldreda holding a model of the monastery at Ely.

Address 14 Ely Place, EC1N 6RY, +44 (0)207 405 1061, www.stetheldreda.com | Getting there Mainline to Farringdon (Thameslink); Tube to Chancery Lane (Central Line), Farringdon (Circle, Hammersmith & City and Metropolitan Lines); Overground to Farringdon; bus: 8, 25, 242, 390 or 521 | Hours Mon–Sat 8am–5pm, Sun 8am–12.30pm, closed bank holidays | Tip Five minutes' walk away is Smithfield, where there are cafés and restaurants. You can also visit Charterhouse (see ch. 19), St Bartholomew the Less (see ch. 23) and the peculiarly named Bleeding Heart Restaurant, from a legend about a lady about town. She was killed in the yard in 1646 by one of her lovers. Some say her ghost still wanders around the yard. There is also the Mitre Tavern, in Ely Court, frequented by Dr Johnson.

52 St John the Baptist
Stunning Anglo-Catholic decoration

Although the church is located on a busy main road, stand on the other side and first admire the rose window and the buttresses, which make the building look very much like the west front of a French Gothic church.

A church where you can see the colourful ritual and gestural drama of Anglo-Catholicism. A church built following the reintroduction of Catholic churches and completed in full, which was not the case with many churches that were purpose built in the 19th century for Catholic congregations. On entering the space, you can follow in the footsteps of what would have been the journey towards the high altar, starting with the wise and foolish virgins – small stone statues either side of the inner west door. But which look wise and which unwise? Clue: the unwise ones are on the north side. In comparison, the mosaics in the church (costing £50 each) of the *Road to Calvary*, cost only £5 each. But this must not be taken to mean anything of course! The 'Devon' marble font (J. S. Adkins) to the left as you enter the church has *quatrefoil* panels on it relating to sacraments such as Baptism, Confirmation, Holy Communion and Penance, looking rather like Ghiberti's famous Florentine bronze Baptistry doors for which he won the famous competition (1401). Adkins also designed the exquisite mosaics.

The *pièce de résistance* is the sculpted screen, topped by archangels (Raphael, Michael, Gabriel and Uriel), accompanied by smaller angels carrying the symbols of the Passion and unusually two screens to either side, which are also decorated with statues.

As late as the 20th century, the church records show that 8,000 communicants had been received in just one week. And not only would people have had a lot of gorgeous materials to gaze at, their knowledge of the Holy hierarchy could increase with all the religious characters displayed throughout the church.

Address Holland Road, W14 8AH, +44 (0)203 602 9873, www.hollandparkbenefice.org |
Getting there Mainline to Shepherds Bush (Southern), Olympia (Southern); Tube to
Shepherds Bush or Holland Park (Central Line); Overground to Sheperhds Bush or
Olympia; bus: 49, 237, 316 or C1 | Hours Mon–Thu 10am–4pm and on Sun for services |
Tip The church has an attractive small café and community space attached.

53__St James

A quirky square for a location

A church dating from 1875 in a non-perfect square, in a non-perfect location, but all the same it has a lot of charm. It has appeal because it shows how, if there is a will, the historical can survive harmoniously with encroaching modernity. And how both old and new can provide something architecturally rich, even if they might seem to jar. Here, though, it works. Such building juxtapositions contribute to London's fascination.

See the beautiful Victorian almshouse building opposite, around which are rows of Georgian terraces, a block of flats or two, including the nearby Packington Estate, seen as a model for new types of housing, both social and private. And Pophams Bakery, which opens at 7.30am, and sells the most delicious pastries. What could be more delightful than having breakfast in the café before visiting a church?

Even though this might feel like a modern Catholic church, on the wall behind the altar are the words of the prayer *Our Father,* and words from the *Book of Exodus* and the *Creed.* The Protestants favoured a return to the word, and quite often post-Reformation churches had such tables. Yet, these were not actually put in until 1875 at a time when Catholicism was being revived.

Find the stained glass containing *grisaille* figures, which was moved from the Lamb chapel in the original church in Monkwell Street, near the old Roman wall in the City. *Grisaille* is a form of painting made to look like or imitate stone. So, the colours are usually muted and grey. The church belonged to the clothworkers and a Mr Lamb was the master clothworker from 1569 (see his memorial above the west door). In the manner of exchange that was one way to get recognised once you had died, he requested that the workers attend one service a year, wearing their livery gowns. At the same time, shoes for 12 poor men and 12 poor women had to be distributed, like a type of dole.

Address Prebend Street, N1 8PF, +44 (0)207 226 4108, www.stjamesislington.org | **Getting there** Mainline to Essex Road (Northern City Line); Tube to Angel (Northern Line); bus: 38, 56, 73, 271, 341 or 476 | **Hours** Daily 10am—6pm, also Sun services at 11am and 4pm | **Tip** The church is not far from the shops and cafés in Islington.

54__Wesley Chapel
Brothers and hymns

Here in the heart of the tech industry, set back from the road, in a cobbled courtyard garden with trees, is the Wesley Chapel. There is a statue of John Wesley holding a small hymn book. Along with his brother, Charles, John devoted his life to finding a new way to worship that spoke to the poor in 18th-century Britain. The brothers wanted a return to reading the Gospel, the practice of Bible study and prayer. From 1738, they became preachers in churches and outdoor spaces and encouraged good work. They also wrote thousands of hymns, many of which are still sung today. The foundation of the Wesleyan movement coincided with an emergence of evangelical spiritual renewal in Europe, where it was realised people's needs were not being met. Built in the classical style, the building has fluted columns framing the portal and five round headed windows above

There are two chapels. The main chapel has the proportions of a church (1778, George Dance the Younger). It is galleried and, significantly, the raised pulpit, so important for Wesleyan preaching, is in the middle towards the east end. There is a low communion rail here, donated by Margaret Thatcher who was married here in 1951. The space has lots of memorials and tablets to former chapel ministers, such as Samuel Danks Waddy, a county court judge. Some of the ministers are memorialised in classical bust form, such as the spectacled William Fiddian Moulton (d. 1898). There is a moving stained glass memorial to World War I: Christ embraces a soldier, kneeling before him, with one bare leg. The smaller Foundry Chapel is an intimate panelled space with stained glass in the ceiling and even a small organ.

Outside, is a small garden, with a memorial to Wesley, below which are his remains. A modern glass building surrounds the garden and some of the gravestones of other ministers have been absorbed by a new courtyard entrance.

Address 49 City Road, EC1Y 1AU, +44 (0)207 253 2262, www.wesleyschapel.org.uk |
Getting there Mainline to Old Street (Great Northern), Liverpool Street (Greater Anglia);
Tube to Old Street (Northern Line, exit 4), Moorgate (Circle, Metropolitan and Northern
Lines); bus: 21, 43, 55, 76, 141, 205, 214, 243 or 271 | Hours Mon–Sat 10am–4pm, Sun
12.30–1.45pm for worship, closed Thu 12.45–1.30pm for worship | Tip The site also has a
small museum dedicated to the history of Methodism. Directly opposite on the other side of
the road is Bunhill Fields, a wonderful burial ground where you will find the gravestones of
William Blake and George Fox.

55__St Agnes
Lambs make peace

Fancy being a mystery church worshipper? St Agnes is one of about 3,000 churches that has been subjected to satirical scrutiny by a mystery worshipper, who visits the church during a service and comments on things such as pew comfort and whether the sermon or the refreshments are any good. Their report is then written up on a website initiative founded in 1998 called the Ship of Fools.

The simple, plain red brick exterior is paralleled by sharp and clean lines inside. The west end has a striking large Gothic-shaped window, redolent of its late 19th-century past. The clarity and simplicity are mirrored in the way in which the post and lintel system of the north entrance is marked by a combination of standard and thin bricks and even two statue-less niches. The church was originally built by George Gilbert Scott, and rebuilt by Ralph Covell (1911–88). He was also an organist at St Agnes.

St Agnes' attribute is a lamb (a sacrificial Christian animal) and you will see an image of her on the west front of the church. She is a beacon of peace against a turbulent life fighting for chastity over marriage. Refusing to marry a Roman governor in the 4th century, he would not take 'no' for an answer and so made her walk naked in the streets. Determined not to give in, the governor then tried to burn her at the stake, which she also survived. Further trials resulted in her being beheaded. Violent treatment for a figure who prioritised peace!

Allow yourself to be tempted and look over the road to Kennington Park and you might just see her with her lamb sitting on the grass, quietly speaking out for women.

Likewise, the church has had a turbulent history. For when it was first built, there was mob protest and despair over the desire to practise using the Catholic liturgy at a time when Catholicism was trying to make a comeback.

Address St Agnes Place, Kennington Park, SE11 4BB, +44 (0)207 820 8050, www.stagneskenningtonpark.co.uk | **Getting there** Tube to Kennington (Northern Line), Oval (Northern Line), Elephant and Castle (Bakerloo and Northern Lines); bus: 133, 145 or 415 | **Hours** During services on Sunday, check the website | **Tip** Opposite is the small, but charming Kennington Park, where you will see an attractive house with the sign *Trees for Life Outside*, while on the other side is the Oval cricket ground.

56_St John the Divine

Loved by John Betjeman

A Victorian church to the design of George Edmund Street (1871–74) who developed polychromy (the 'streaky bacon style'). See the pointed apertures on the tower, the red brick contrasting with the stone dressings and articulations, the apse's exterior looking a little like a small beehive and the rose garden courtyard to the left of the north entrance. With the interior's vaulted apse, here is Victorian architecture resembling Byzantine and Romanesque church designs. Part of the high altar painting is in the shape of an oval or more commonly in art history parlance an almond (a *mandorla*). Deliberate or not, the church is close to the Oval cricket ground.

Look at the colourful, high-relief *Road to Calvary* sculptures, by Mother Maribel, exhibiting facial expressions of grief and anguish to witness Christ dragging the cross up to Golgotha. The faces do not feature as prominently as the body types: bent, huddled, stretched, convoluted and twisted, illustrating the pain of this event. The cross is set at an angle or semi elevated from a horizontal position in the 12 different scenes. It looks as though it is pushing out into our space. And the heavy mood is highlighted in how exhausted Christ looks. There are Roman soldiers nailing him to the cross wearing bright turquoise leggings. The series succeeds in showing all that carrying, heaving and struggling through suffering. There are, for example three panels of 'Christ falling down'.

The large bronze statue ensemble – the *Crucifixion, The Kelham Rood* (1929) is by Charles Jagger. Here is John and a mourning Virgin below. While John is usually seen standing straight supporting Mary at the Crucifixion scene, he is bent (as are so many figures in this church) with both his hands on his face, obscuring it completely. By contrast, Mary's face is exposed; her arms are outstretched towards the figure of Christ.

Address 92 Vassall Road, Kennington, SW9 6JA, +44 (0)207 735 9340, www.sjdk.org |
Getting there Tube to Oval (Northern Line); bus: 3, 36, 59, 133, 155 or 159 | Hours
Mon–Fri 3–6pm, term time, and during service times | Tip Afterwards you can go to
Myatt's Field Park, where there is the Little Cat Café, with outdoor seating for the summer.

57 _ St Mark

Coptic Orthodox in Kensington

This must be one of the most beautiful church interiors in London, for it glitters and dazzles with light and rich colours, radiating from the stained glass and the icons. It feels a bit like visiting a secret garden. From small London streets, you are transported into exotic realms. That precious feeling is enhanced as you enter through a narrow portal. The exterior, essentially London Gothic, with pointed windows and tracery, does not prepare you for what is found within. While the feel of a slightly gloomy London church interior is still felt, that is altered by the presence of the icons and other images, such as that of the dedicatee saint, St Mark.

The church's website calls itself 'the mother of all Coptic Orthodox churches in the United Kingdom'. And it was opened as a Coptic church in 1973, the first in Europe. The word *Coptic* is the Greek word for Egypt, so this is a church with ancient and eastern roots and connections, which brings home to us that the origins of Christianity come from the Middle East.

It is thought that St Mark founded the Coptic church. And the head of this church is known as the 'Patriarch of Alexandria on the Holy See of Saint Mark'. It is believed that Mark travelled to Alexandria in c. 49CE and founded the Coptic Orthodox church there. He has another claim to fame. In 828, his body was stolen from Alexandria and ended up in Venice. His relics, apart from his head, allegedly in Cairo, are preserved in the Basilica of San Marco in Venice.

On the exterior's corner buttress, there is an image in vivid colours of the saint in the act of writing his Gospel. Previously, the church belonged to the Presbyterian church dating from 1863, which followed on from residential development in Scarsdale Villas from 1854–64; so its appearance now must be very different from how 19th-century residents of this area would remember the church.

Address Allen Street, off High Street Kensington, W8 6UX, +44 (0)7956 855 334, www.stmark.org.uk | Getting there Tube to High Street Kensington (Circle and District Lines); bus: 9, 10 or 27 | Hours Daily, reasonable hours | Tip The magnificent Leighton House, home and studio of Lord Leighton, a leading Victorian artist, is close by on Holland Park Road (www.rbkc.gov.uk).

58 St Mary Abbots

Flight into Egypt

Just off the busy Kensington High Street is a covered walkway/cloister to the south of the church. On the north side of the building are paths that take you to beauty salons and florists where one rose alone costs £20. After all, this is Kensington, containing some of the most expensive London houses ever built. The church dates to 1000CE when it was founded by an abbot from Abingdon. By the time it was rebuilt by George Gilbert Scott (1872), who also designed the Albert Memorial (not far from here), the neighbourhood was inhabited by aristocrats. No doubt their days were occupied having afternoon tea in heavily draped parlours or drinking brandy wearing velvet jackets and slippers.

The church has a notable sculpture inside that is easily missed. This is the *Holy Family fleeing for Safety and Refuge*, made in 1972 by Marjorie Crossley. Joseph, Mary and Jesus became refugees when Herod sent his soldiers to massacre the innocent children, with mothers pleading for their lives, but to no avail. The subject is drawn from the *Gospel of St Matthew* (2: 13 – 15) which gives only a brief account of the departure of the Holy Family from Bethlehem after Joseph's dream in which an angel warns him of what is about to happen. The journey took place by night. Here, we see a donkey who transports the load: Joseph walking beside and Mary and the baby Jesus riding side-saddle. A close-knit group, where the folds of their clothes mingle, making limb and form less discernible, but which enhances the tension of their bodies. Joseph holds his walking staff, Mary tightly clasps her baby, one hand on his knees and bent legs, the other hand wrapped around his back to hold him. She is not going to let her baby go. Jesus is haloed, but his parents are not.

The sculptural group is a moving and poignant reminder of the world's recent refugee crisis.

Address Kensington Church Street, W8 4LA, +44 (0)207 937 5136, www.smaw8.org |
Getting there Tube to High Street Kensington (Circle and District Lines), Notting Hill
Gate (Central Line); bus: 9, 10, 27, 28, 49, 52, 70, 328, 452 or C1 | **Hours** Mon–Fri
7.30am–6pm, Sat 9am 6pm, Sun 7am–7.45pm | **Tip** Kensington Palace and Gardens
are just moments away.

59__St Silas the Martyr
The best church website in town

St Silas church was built by Ernest Charles Shearman (1911–13), who, according to the encyclopaedic website was a 'bachelor when he married aged 26'. He also designed the altar candlesticks and a Crucifix for the church. The dedicatee saint is not St Silas Abba, an Italian noble found dead in the bushes under his 'chamber window'. We do not know whether he was using his chamber pot when he died. No, the correct St Silas for this church was an early Christian missionary saint, 'chief men among the Brethren', along with Judas Barnabus (*Acts* 15: 1–29). There is a statue of him inside the church, holding a ship and with mitre and cope. Do not miss what he is standing on!

Here is an adorable church in his remembrance with rather fine proportions, tucked away down a little cul-de-sac. There are other statues of less well-known saints such as Norbert, John Vianney, John Nepomuk and Gerard Majella. Visit the St Francis chapel with stained glass by Henry Victor Milner (1866–1944), who used grey glass to echo the habits of the Franciscan Order. His studio, ironically, was opposite the Dominican Priory (see ch. 47).

The building has a high-pitched roof: a little bit of Paris. Notably, the church has no tower or spire. See the corbels at the entrance – with busts of St Joan of Arc and St George solemnly staring out. To the right is a stone *Crucifixion* and on the left a carving of one of the centurions witnessing the event. The church was consecrated on Saturday, 26 October, 1912 by the Bishop of London, the Right Reverend Arthur Foley Winnington-Ingram – a name to treasure and memorise. Such wonderful information is found on the church's website – which should be awarded first prize. It contains vintage photographs of mystery plays performed here in the early 20th century, and short biographies of figures associated with the church such as T. S. Eliot, who took confession here.

Address St Silas Place, off Prince of Wales Road, NW5 3QP, +44 (0)207 485 3727, www.saintsilas.org.uk | Getting there Tube to Chalk Farm (Northern Line); bus: 24 or 46 | Hours Daily, three times a day, check on the website | Tip The church is close to the Zabludowicz Collection, a contemporary art gallery (www.zabludowiczcollection.com).

60 St Augustine

Hours and hours of time to gaze required

Before this church was built, local congregations sympathetic to the Oxford Movement went on a specially chartered omnibus to other churches such as St Cyprian (see ch. 1) or St Mary Magdalene Paddington (see ch. 75). This changed, when a determined Reverend Richard Carr Kirkpatrick established the church in this magnificent space (begun 1871 and consecrated in 1880). He had been assistant curate at St Mary, Kilburn, where his Anglo-Catholic practices were suppressed.

The church has a bold, long nave and large ambulatory, which is an area of the church behind the altar, at the east end. You can walk around the ambulatory, as the name deriving from the Latin *ambulare*, to walk, suggests. Such a design enables you to look back at the body of the church from a different angle. The architect was John Loughborough Pearson (see ch. 8). Sir Giles Gilbert Scott (1880–1960), the architect and designer, designed the Madonna and Child and the *Stations of the Cross* and the *reredos* in the Lady Chapel.

The word ornate sums up much of the church. Indeed, the Lady Chapel, the chapel to St Michael, the church's colours, the array of materials, ravishing light and vistas have resulted in many plaudits from architectural critics. Although the strange and grotesque lurk as well.

The iconography in the church can be read almost as a programme of reading about figures and scenes from the *Old* to the *New Testaments*. At the west end rose window are stories from the Creation, the Fall of Man and Moses delivering the tablets of the Law, with Jesus in the centre. In the aisles are windows of saints including St Dunstan of Canterbury and St Edward the Confessor. Female saints are opposite – St Hilda, St Winifred, abbess of Holy Well and St Helena. Perhaps not surprisingly the vision of the *New Testament* continues towards the east on the Rood screen and in the chancel in stone.

Address Kilburn Park Road, NW6 5XD, +44 (0)207 624 1637, www.saugustinekilburn.org | Getting there Tube to Kilburn Park Road (Bakerloo Line); bus: 31, 32, 206 or 316 | Hours Sat 9am–3.15pm (check website), Sun 7.30–8.45am, 9.45am–12.30pm, masses at 8am & 10.30am | Tip 15 minutes' walk away is Little Venice, a charming part of London to wander around in.

61 __ Cathedral of the Dormition

Don't judge a church by its exterior

Tucked away in a little street south of Kensington Gardens is a gorgeous church interior. It is a sensual, glorious multicoloured space with gold at every turn. This is the Russian Orthodox church of Knightsbridge (1848–49, Lewis Vulliamy).

The exterior has a rose window and a classical looking front. There is a tripartite façade with a simple pediment at the top of the central section, and a few rounded arches to break up the mass of stone. And with a tower as well, there are many features that you might associate with the plain unadorned exteriors of Venetian churches. Indeed, the front was designed by Charles Harrison Townsend in 1892, who also did the wonderful Horniman Museum. None of this appearance prepares you for the interior.

Inside, the hues are golden, lemony, honey like, peach and apricot, glowing all at once. An expressive effect caught by the shimmering effects of colour and light made by a glut of materials. There is a striking altar screen and above a gold coloured apse of great majesty. The emphasis is on strident visual material, coupled with the inclusion of figurative imagery in the icons.

Why such a contrast between the exterior and the interior? Well, because originally the church was a parish church for the community, and when the Russian Orthodox community took over the church in 1979, the interior was completely transformed.

There are icons on small high tables, both on the right and on the left of the nave. Some of the icons' sacredness is lit by thin, tapering candles, which are commonly for sale in Orthodox churches. Above is a massive chandelier. So there is some candlelight and some electricity, resulting in a magical setting. On the floor by these icon settings are some metal oval shaped bowls, with a very important function.

Address 67 Ennismore Gardens, SW7 1NH, +44 (0)207 584 0096, www.sourozh.org | Getting there Tube to South Kensington (Circle and District Lines), Knightsbridge (Piccadilly Line); bus: 9, 10, 52 or 452 | Hours Daily 9am–8pm but best not to visit on Sun mornings when services are on | Tip All the museums in South Kensington are very close.

62 St Mary-at-Lambeth

Plants, tombs and objects

A church and museum full of gardening implements, sketchbooks, seed packets, postcards and paintings of gardens and gardeners. You can climb the medieval tower; there are tracery windows and clean white stones. On a mezzanine level, you can get really close to a stained glass window and openings from above have been made, so you can look down on the nave. And the space itself has lots of nooks and crannies. The church is not only the neighbour of the River Thames, but it has a lovely garden, with box hedges, pots and mosaics where the plants weave in and out of the tombs. One is of the botanist, James Sowerby (1757–1822); he illustrated a magazine run by William Curtis who had a botanical garden where Waterloo station is today. And there is a café facing onto greenery and more stones. There is even a place to park your bike. Although, once long ago, the only way to cross to this church from the north was on the horse ferry.

Edward the Confessor's sister Goda built the original church. And the medieval foundations have a 'neat' connection to gardening, as the first recorded gardener was 'Edmund the Gardener' – gardener to King Edward I at Windsor Castle. And John Tradescant the Younger (1608–62) gardener to Queen Henrietta Maria (wife of Charles I) and his father, also called John (c. 1570–1638), are commemorated in a room dedicated to the fashion then for a cabinet of curiosities. There are two tombs and a statue of St Fiacre, patron saint of gardening.

Note the *Pedlar's Window* by Francis Stephens (1921–2002), in the Walcot Room. It is thought the figure represented is a parish boy who, according to a legend, was given the right to bury his dog in a churchyard rather than in a ditch. So the boy, doing the right thing, later gave money back to the church.

Look for the rare immersion font, where you walk down some steps below the church to be baptised.

Address Lambeth Palace Road, SE1 7LB, +44 (0)207 401 8865, www.gardenmuseum.org.uk | Getting there Mainline to Waterloo (South Western) and Waterloo East (Southeastern); Tube to Waterloo (Waterloo & City, Jubilee and Northern Lines), Westminster (Circle, District and Jubilee Lines), Lambeth North (Bakerloo Line); bus: 3, 59, 68, 159 or 322 | Hours Mon–Fri 10.30am–5pm, Sat 10.30am–4pm, open on bank holidays excluding Christmas Day, Boxing Day and New Year's Day and the first Mon of the month | Tip You can also visit Lambeth Palace, but only on guided tours and Garden Open Days (archbishopofcanterbury.org).

63 __ St Margaret
Choreography of the Arts and Crafts Movement

The Arts and Crafts Movement (c. 1860–1920) sought to revive manual artistic work and processes that were thought to have been forgotten during what was seen, by some, as the ugly advance of industrialisation. You can see the sort of visual appearance adopted by the movement in this building (dating from 1875). A church to savour with its surface decoration and imagery and nothing left blank or white. Although when the church was first built, it was all white and lasted this way for 20 years.

The interior preserves the work of a unified cohort of craftspeople. Much of the work was paid for by one Lady Adelaide Law. You will see her good taste and a grand ambition for things. The interior has light, and colour, space and height. But there is another reason why you need lots of time to visit, and that is because you will be met by three charming volunteers, all keen to share their love of the church with you. Except for Sunday services, the church opens only on one Saturday a month for visits, so it feels special indeed.

The church is awash with painted narratives, many of Christian saints such as St Margaret with her dragon. We can also read some church history in the stained glass windows (made by the famous firm of Clayton and Bell, as in King's College, Cambridge) – such as the *Magna Carta* recording that the Manor of Lee was held by Richard de Mountfichet. The church is also full of specialist painting techniques, such as *marouflage* in the nave, and of particular note are the carved holy figures on the altar table, done by Violet Pinwill (1874–1957), whose father, a rector, encouraged three of his daughters to possess a skill. She ended up making carvings for around 200 churches all over the United Kingdom.

While many churches are an accretion of layers and many different styles, here instead, you see a carefully planned, coordinated interior design scheme.

Address Lee Terrace, SE13 5DL, +44 (0)208 318 9643, www.stmargaretslee.org.uk |
Getting there Mainline to Blackheath (Southeastern); bus: 54, 89, 108, 185 or 261 | Hours
First Sat of the month, 10.30am–4.30pm, or on Sun at service times | Tip Edmond Halley
is buried in the churchyard. Also over the road is the Boone chapel (1682) belonging to the
estate of Lee Place and where there were once almshouses. An authentic ice house is nearby,
which was once part of the Manor House.

64 Notre Dame de France

The minimalist art of Jean Cocteau

Notre Dame is located on a pedestrian street in Soho, just north of Leicester Square. Built in 1861, it is the place of worship for French-speaking people in the heart of London.

Jean Cocteau (1889–1963), an avant-garde painter, poet, playwright and filmmaker of the early 20th century, decorated the Lady Chapel in November 1959 with a remarkable ability to paint minimalist line and colour. Here are murals dedicated to the Virgin Mary and show the *Annunciation*, the *Crucifixion* and the *Assumption of the Virgin Mary*. They are so simple, fresh and authentic that you might wonder if the artist is coming back to continue to paint. Trace with your eyes the curvaceous lines he has made, which could result in rather amorphous shapes, but instead create an ethereal quality fitting for the figures he was depicting. If you know that he only painted these in a week, you might not be surprised at their understated quality. But if he had been given longer, the effect may not have been the same. It is said that he lit a candle before the statue of *Our Lady of Lourdes* every morning when he came into paint. See if you can find where his self-portrait is! Christian art has a long-standing tradition of the inclusion of patron and/or artist in a commissioned work. While we might think such an act rather audacious, it has always been quite the norm.

In the side chapel, see the altar mosaic of the *Nativity* (1954) by Boris Anrep (1885–1969), a Russian artist who also did mosaics at other London institutions such as Westminster Cathedral, and in the sanctuary of another church worth visiting – the Greek cathedral of Saint Sophia in Bayswater.

Vision plays a strong part in the current church, but also its history. It stands where once was a legendary panorama (1793, Robert Barker) of 10,000 square feet and a viewing platform, which also explains the round shape of the church.

Address 5 Leicester Place, WC2H 7BX, +44 (0)207 437 9363, www.ndfchurch.org/en |
Getting there Tube to Leicester Square (Northern and Piccadilly Lines); bus: 23, 24, 29
or 176 | Hours Daily 9am–9pm | Tip For other images of Christ and the Virgin Mary to
compare with the Cocteau images, you can walk through Leicester Square and visit the
National Gallery.

65__St Mary

A place for graffiti, brasses, urns and bodies

What is it about some church spaces that seems to take you back into the mists of time without you knowing when that time is? St Mary's fits that bill. Enter via the churchyard with bent, old, gravestones and equally old knotted blossom trees. A church that you might imagine more fitting in the depths of the Dorset countryside than here in downtown Ilford. This church sits like a fragile stone in the middle of a large residential area. Yet the church itself is durable and solid with walls up to three feet thick. Here are Norman foundations and the feel is one of permanence.

The church is rich in historical fragments. Roman stones at the structure's foundations, medieval graffiti in the form of the odd witch's mark (two enclosed, or interlocking 'W' marks), and a crypt with 'viscera coffins' down there, complete with body parts. These are associated with the Lethieullier family whose chapel on the north side of the nave contains the family vault below (dated to 1737). The family were local, and John Lethieullier was a trader, a merchant adventurer and mentioned by Samuel Pepys in his diaries. His son, Smart, sent bodies to the British Museum for exhibition and display, along with artefacts collected on the Grand Tour. The family used the chapel extensively on a Sunday, beginning with the morning service and staying until the 3pm evensong. A little fireplace that presumably kept them warm can still be seen. In the chapel window is a tiny fragment of stained glass, thought to be of 16th–17th-century Netherlandish origin. It is a fragment of the *Deposition of Christ*.

You will see the brass of young Thomas Heron (died aged 14), shown standing up, with inkhorn and pencil case hanging from his belt. His younger brother, Giles, married Cecily, the younger daughter of Sir Thomas More. Of note too is the beautiful rectors' board made by Francis Donkin Bedford (1896).

Address Church Road, Manor Park, E12 6HA, www.achurchnearyou.com | **Getting there** Mainline to Manor Park (Great Eastern Mainline); Overground to Woodgrange Park; Tube to East Ham (District and Hammersmith & City Lines), bus: 25, 147 or W19 | **Hours** By arrangement and on Open Days | **Tip** Afterwards, visit the stunning Hindu temple (www.londonsrimurugan.org). Smart Lethieullier knew William John Hunter whose collections are housed at the Hunterian Medical Museum in Lincoln's Inn Fields.

66 St James' Spanish Place

Materials in Heaven

A large and beautiful Catholic church (consecrated 1949) which is open most of the day. The exterior of grey, cold looking stone with buttresses is quite forbidding but do not be put off; go inside and you will find an interior rather like a bewitching medieval cathedral. The church was originally a chapel for the Spanish Embassy and was first located where the Wallace Collection is now. As Catholics in London became more confident about establishing spaces again, what we see today is a confident statement to support the 5,000 Catholics living in the area in the 19th century.

As you might expect, the church commemorates its dedicatee saint – look out for the elegant marble statue of St James, one of the first four Apostles called by Christ, who were fishermen, with the characteristic sword and palm denoting his martyrdom. But he also carries a staff and a 'bread wallet' to record him as the patron saint of pilgrimage. His relics, part of an elaborate shrine, are at the cathedral at Santiago de Compostela in northern Spain, still an important pilgrimage destination.

At the altar is an altar frontal, painted in a striking fine ceramic technique, which you can use to identify saints. See if you can pick out St Thomas Aquinas, St Francis and St John the Baptist. Instead of the conventional gold leaf, each saint has a pearly halo on them – a link to the pearly kings and queens of London's East End!

Look at the picture by Geoffrey Webb of some of the English Martyrs (1535–1679) executed at Tyburn, as they rejected Protestantism at the time of the Reformation and beyond. The man in blue holding an oar was a Thames Lighterman. In a side chapel, on St Joseph's altar, you will see the subject of the *Flight into Egypt,* made by John Francis Bentley (1839–1902), who specialised in religious architecture, and was also the architect of Westminster Cathedral.

Address 22 George Street, W1U 3QY, +44 (0)207 935 0943, www.sjrcc.org.uk | Getting there Mainline to Marylebone (Chiltern Railways); Tube to Marylebone (Bakerloo Line), Baker Street (Bakerloo, Hammersmith & City, Jubilee and Metropolitan Lines), Bond Street (Central Line); bus: 13, 30, 113 or 139 | Hours Daily 7am–7pm | Tip The Wallace Collection is opposite the church in Manchester Square and has a lovely setting for a café (www.wallacecollection.org).

67_ The Swedish Church
Cinnamon buns and coffee

The Swedish Church, known as The Ulrika Eleonora Swedish Parish, beckons with the sign of coffee within. Ulrika Eleonora was the Queen of Sweden from 1718 to 1720, who, at one time, may have become the wife of King George II and was profoundly religious.

Although a buzzer needs to be pressed to enter, this church is open for business and is most hospitable, as witnessed not only by the welcoming sign, but the community centre and the café. You might be greeted with the word *Hej,* the Swedish for 'hello.'

The church interior has some wonderfully designed lights. You might notice that the embroidered hassocks here are thinner than usual, possibly done to give people a harder time of it as they knelt on the floor. Yet, you will notice that the space and furnishings are pared down and offer a quintessential Nordic space, or at least how we tend to regard that design aesthetic. Somehow, this might seem in keeping with the Swedish approach to worship, as the church follows the Lutheran form. Although that is not to say that after the Reformation they abandoned priestly garments and the Mass. The Reformation offered all sorts of nuances to the way forward with liturgy and faith. Ritual and elaborate celebration still have a place here. And the space within is large and majestic.

You will notice, for example, that the altar screen is ornate and gilded. Below is a *Last Supper* with the words *Gud Ar Karlek* (God is Love). The rose window shimmers with reflecting light from outside. In the interior vestibule note the beautifully drawn flower rota. The church objects are artfully placed. Ikea was not born out of nothing.

Every year the church organises a Christmas market where you can buy Swedish goods: candles, buns and decorations.

Originally, the Swedish Church was in Wapping (from 1728); the present church contains furnishings from the original interior.

Address 6 Harcourt Street, W1H 4HG, +44 (0)207 723 5681, www.svenskakyrkan.se/london | **Getting there** Mainline to Marylebone (Chiltern Railways); Tube to Marylebone (Bakerloo Line), Baker Street (Circle, Hammersmith & City and Metropolitan Lines); bus: 13, 16, 98, 189 or 205 | **Hours** Mon, Tue, Fri & Sat 10am–5pm, Wed 10am–7pm, Sun noon–3pm | **Tip** You might also like to visit the other Nordic churches in London: the Danish, Finnish, Icelandic and Norwegian churches.

68___Grosvenor Chapel
A sculpture and a door all in one

The original benefactor, Sir Richard Grosvenor, owned the surrounding property and land. The chapel (completed in 1731, designed by Benjamin Timbrell), is situated not far from Grosvenor Square, the largest residential square in London.

Look out for the brightly painted blue doors within the little portico topped by a lintel, adjoining the tower. The result is one of elegance, proportion and symmetry, and in keeping with the classical principles of architecture that the structure exhibits. There is even a graceful volute to accentuate the edge of the central section, above a gently carved pediment. The pleasing regularity of the exterior is mirrored inside, which is enticingly light and white. It has a similar feel to St George's in Hanover Square. That may have been a good thing for the 19th-century parishioner, as from 1829 the chapel became a chapel of ease to St George's.

It is worth looking at the nave memorial door (2018) funded by and dedicated to Robert Frederick Goldhammer (1931–2014), a businessman and philanthropist who worshipped here. In the *tympanum* of the door is a charming relief sculpture in gold, which has no back and so the space is transparent, letting in light to the nave and out again, a wonderful reflection of how one of the functions of a church space was to let in the light of God. The sculpture was made by Alexander Stoddart, the Queen's Sculptor in Ordinary in Scotland. It depicts Christ meeting his mother in Heaven after his Resurrection, a sort of *Coronation of the Virgin*. Mary kneels before Christ, while holding out her left hand as if to touch his gesturing right hand. She is by a lectern and an open book, just as we often see her in Annunciation scenes. They both stand against a portico that echoes the portico of the actual entrance to the chapel.

It might be worth noting that the church has a 'Hymns and Pimms Co-ordinator'.

Address 24 South Audley Street, Mayfair, W1K 2PA, +44 (0)207 499 1684, www.grosvenorchapel.org.uk | Getting there Crossrail to Bond Street; Tube to Bond Street (Central Line), Green Park (Jubilee and Victoria Lines); bus: 16, 36, 73, 82, 148, 414 or 436 | Hours Mon–Fri 8am–5pm & Sun 8am–2pm | Tip A 5-minute walk will take you to Hyde Park Gardens and the Serpentine Art Gallery.

69 St George Hanover Square
A 50 Churches Act church (1711)

The church was built by John James (1721–24). He succeeded Wren as surveyor to St Paul's Cathedral. The *50 Churches Act* was an Act of Parliament set up to build lots of new churches to cope with the increasing urbanism and population of London in the early 18th century. Many of the churches were built by Nicholas Hawksmoor, such as his famous Christchurch, Spitalfields. They were paid for by a duty on coal coming into London. James built some of St Alfege in Greenwich (see ch. 42) and built a house, for James Johnson, secretary of state for Scotland.

As an early 18th-century building, this is an interior that reflects the interest in classical architecture during this time, such as square piers carrying columns with capitals (gilded). It has elegance and eloquence, light and balance, and encapsulates just what is so timeless about the model of classical antiquity.

At the east end at the *reredos* is a *Last Supper* by William Kent (1685–1748), who evidently was a bit of a polymath in the true Renaissance tradition, with skills in architecture, landscape gardening, furniture design and painting. We can also see the influence of Netherlandish art in the 16th-century stained glass by Arnold of Nijmegen (c. 1490–1536) brought over from a church in Antwerp, but which was only placed in St George's in the 1840s. He did work in Rouen and Tournai Cathedral, but it took a while for his fame to extend to Britain; even though Henry VIII commissioned Low Countries artists to paint for him, but not, surprisingly, this exceptional designer.

Handel, who lived not far away in Brook Street from 1723 to 1759 (see Handel House Museum), auditioned organists at the church. Benjamin Disraeli, Theodore Roosevelt and George Eliot were all married here. Indeed, it has always been a popular venue for nuptials. In 1816 alone, the church officiated over 1,000 weddings.

Address Hanover Square, W1S 1FX, +44 (0)207 629 0874, www.stgeorgeshanoversquare.org | Getting there Tube to Oxford Circus (Central Line), Piccadilly Circus (Bakerloo and Piccadilly Lines), Bond Street (Central Line), Green Park (Jubilee and Victoria Lines); Crossrail to Bond Street; bus 12, 94, 98, 113, 139, 390 or 453 | Hours Sun 8am–noon | Tip The church is near Berkeley Square, one of London's most famous squares, and you can also visit the Catholic Church of the Immaculate Conception in Farm Street with a high altar designed by Pugin.

70__St James

An artist's notes on how to care for a mural

At the high altar is a Hans Feibusch (1898–1998) mural consisting of the *Resurrection*, with *Noli me Tangere* to the left and the *Road to Emmaus* on the right. Christ appears in all three images, but looks slightly different in each scene.

Note the clump of leaves at the foot of the archway in the *Resurrection*, which are arum lilies. Feibusch had seen these in the sanctuary and was inspired to use them in his composition. At Easter, Miss K. Dora Rendell, then responsible for flowers in the church, decided 'to have a glorious display of arum lilies adorned by their own large leaves around the rim (of a large Ali Baba type vase … to stand to the left of the altar), the whole arrangement being crowned by a mass of blue/mauve and purple/pink irises'. Feibusch observed how the green walls of the church and the lilies were so striking, that he opted to make his skyline match that of the iris (it had been a greyish blue). At the time of the dedication of the mural on 28 April, 1958, Feibusch asked Dora if she would make an exact copy of the arrangement she had previously prepared for Easter, and so the leaves at the foot of the archway in the mural are a testament to Dora's flower arrangement!

There is nothing like bringing a work of art to life through the personal accounts of an artist. The church is also fortunate in having a letter from Feibusch to a Mr Gooderick, dated to 16 October, 1975, following a visit the former had made to the church to view his mural. He had clearly been asked to advise on caring for the mural, and that included clearing away 'spots' with washing, not with soap or any other detergent, but just a soft sponge and plenty of fresh water. He added that the water should not run down the wall. Seventeen years later, the artist was still engaged with his previous work and signed off the letter by saying, 'Let me know the result of the operation'.

Address Martin Way, Morden, SM4 4AR, +44 (0)203 016 5156, www.stjames-merton.org.uk | Getting there Mainline to South Merton and Wimbledon (South Western); Tube to Wimbledon (Circle and District Lines); bus: 164 | Hours Any reasonable time on request by appointment, also Sun for services | Tip Not far away is the beautiful conservation area of South Wimbledon.

71__St Michael

A pulsating Devil amidst gold

The church lies at the junction of a tree-lined street and Ladbroke Grove, in a largely residential neighbourhood. The exterior is constructed of brick, with a little bit of terracotta for variety and a few stone dressings to articulate windows around the tower, which also give the building an authentic feel. It was designed by James Edmeston (1791–1867), completed 1871, who was also known as a writer of hymns, including the popular 'Lead us, Heavenly Father, lead us / O'er the world's tempestuous sea'. The apse is distinctive on the outside, with quite a lot of colour added to articulate shapes and windows. Inside, simplicity is replaced by adornment, with quite a lot to deter one.

St Michael's declares itself a Catholic church. You can smell the incense, which is a good enough reason to visit and enjoy the space and transport you somewhere else. Italy, maybe?

St Michael was an archangel. Therefore, he was a suitable figure to be seen often weighing up the goats from the sheep with his scales at the Last Judgement, but also killing devils and dragons who are not wanted in the Christian liturgy. St Michael is often personified as the church militant, true, strong, bold and brave. The grisly Devil, though looking all too human: being trampled upon by the saint in a sculpture near the east end, in a rather ghoulish statue, is accentuated by the gold wings of St Michael. The Devil is clutching onto the angel's red robe as if to beg for mercy.

And by the altar, in a tiny space, is a little chapel, decorated in dense, quite dark colours and then within that, another tiny chapel known as the Walsingham Chapel. This area of the church is cute and the sort of thing that children would love, as one little space leads into another, with various visual distractions along the way. See if you can find the *Adoration of the Magi* stained glass with a cow in the background.

Address 35 St Lawrence Terrace, Ladbroke Grove, W10 5SR, +44 (0)208 969 0776, www.saintmichaelandallangels.com | **Getting there** Tube to Ladbroke Grove (Circle and Hammersmith & City Lines); bus: 7, 52, 70 or 452 | **Hours** Daily, reasonable hours | **Tip** Walk further south and you will eventually get to Portobello Road for its market, shops and restaurants.

72 _ St James Norlands

A church in the middle of a beautiful garden

Here is a church set in its own beautiful garden. If you are lucky enough to visit in the half-light of dusk, with the tentative settling of frost on the trees and a few autumnal golden leaves falling, you might think the church is exclusively for the residents of the square. For there is a digital keypad to enter the church garden. The information board gives one some idea of the difficulties there are in finding the funds to build a church. It declares that 'owing to a lack of funds, the church had only a tower and not a spire.'

Despite this paucity, the area is part of the 18th-century Norland estate, which consists of four-storeyed houses, elegant streets and squares. It was later bought by the watchmaker Benjamin Vulliamy, having grown to 40 acres (see ch. 101). His brother, Lewis Vulliamy, was the architect in charge of the church (begun 1844–55), made of white Suffolk bricks. You will see the gabled porch and the pointed arch framing the window above, which also contains tracery. These are the architectural characteristics of many churches built in the Gothic period.

The interior is majestic with a clerestoried nave and a carved *Last Supper* set into a wooden *reredos* at the east end. Like many churches, the interior would have once been brightly coloured, making what you see today rather sombre in comparison. But the church's garden location, planted with chestnut and lime trees, in this beautiful residential area, gives you some idea of what it would have been like to live in such a London square once upon a time.

St James, the dedicatee saint, is honoured in the pilgrimage to Santiago de Compostela, with the scallop shell symbol often found on pilgrimage bags and hats even to this day. He was with Christ as he prayed towards the end of his life in the Garden of Gethsemane. This makes the setting of the church in this garden rather relevant.

Address St James' Gardens, Notting Hill, W11 4RB, +44 (0)207 221 3548, www.stclementjames.org.uk | **Getting there** Tube to Latimer Road (Hammersmith & City Line), Holland Park (Central Line); bus: 31, 94, 148 or 228 | **Hours** Sun for services or Wed 10.30am for service | **Tip** The Spanish and Portuguese synagogue, with a Byzantine looking exterior, is on St James' Gardens.

73__St John
Christmas begins here

We all know how good the Victorians were at celebrating Christmas. At the 19th-century church of St John the Evangelist, Christmas trees for sale, welcoming Advent, are placed against one of the south transepts.

Inside, all is elegant, spacious, light and radiant, in keeping with a gracious part of London, exclusively sited on a hill. At the time of the church building, this was one of many residential neighbourhoods, like hermetically sealed mini estates replete with an inn and a church for all the gracious homes and hearths.

This church was built on the land owned by the Ladbroke family who acquired the land in the 1700s, when it consisted of fields. The building was completed by 1845 to the design of John Hargrave Stevens and George Alexander. As a parishioner, you had to pay for pew rents (1,100 of them), while only 400 were free. All is sturdy, statuesque and exalted.

In its Victorian heyday, residents in their bonnets and bowler hats would simply cross the road to be reminded of Christ on the cross, where often depictions show St John the Evangelist on one side and Christ's mother, Mary, on the other.

If you stand at the altar and look out before you at the large space, consisting of five bays and many windows, you might imagine the vicar looking out towards the congregation. He or she might point to the sculpture of Christ, as an ordinary man on a donkey. He is dressed in an overall as if he is going to his labouring job – a quotidian 'take' on the *Entry into Jerusalem,* the first part of the Passion narrative, leading up to Christ's death and Crucifixion. As he enters Jerusalem, he is often surrounded by people welcoming him; some even on trees with olive branches, who recognise him as somebody special. But here, he is alone, as if to make him look like one of us.

Address Lansdowne Crescent, Notting Hill Gate, W11 2NN, +44 (0)207 727 4262, bwww.stjohnsnottinghill.com | **Getting there** Tube to Notting Hill Gate (Central Line); bus: 23, 52, 148, 228 or 452 | **Hours** Mon–Fri 8.45am–5.30pm, Sat 8.30am–1pm, Sun 7.30am–6pm; Café Mon–Thu 10am–3pm | **Tip** In 8 minutes you can walk from the church to the lovely Holland Park.

74__St James
Twinning loos

In the church loo is a sign to say that the church twins its toilet with others around the world. It is supporting and in tandem with Latrine no. 10785 in the Congo. What a genius way to connect religious spaces far and wide. And what a way to beckon you into both lavatory and church.

The 19th-century structure consists of a wide nave. You might have fun speaking out loud the guttural sounds of the architects' names – John Goldicutt and George Gutch. The church was then enlarged by George Edmund Street (1824–81) for around 1,300 people to accommodate a growing population. Street, like a lot of builders then, used the Gothic style, notably the arcade with pointed arches. At the large altar is a carving of the *Last Supper*, which is repeated in the stained glass image above. The Last Supper, Christ's last meal in which he participated with the disciples, was a Passover celebration, but for Christians marks the first time that Christ gave the instructions to consecrate his body (the bread) and his blood (the wine).

At the west end of the church is a stained glass window commemorating the Battle of Britain (1940), while below the *Nativity* and the *Crucifixion* are two further scenes of World War II. The local neighbourhood is also commemorated, for example Paddington Station is depicted. The church's location near the Grand Junction canal and then the Great Western Railway (from 1838), was at the heart of trade and transport.

However, St James' foundations go back further. You will see 17th-century engravings of the original medieval church on Paddington Green with stocks outside, showing us that while sin exists, Christianity would forgive.

Robert Stephenson Smyth Baden-Powell, founder of the Scout Movement (1857–1941), was baptised in the church in 1857. And visitors to the church might have included J. M. Barrie (1860–1937).

Address Sussex Gardens, W2 3UD, +44 (0)207 262 9976, www.stjamespaddington.org.uk |
Getting there Tube to Paddington (Circle and District Lines), Lancaster Gate (Circle and
District Lines); bus: 36, 46, 94 or 148 | **Hours** Daily 9.30am – 7.30pm | **Tip** The church is
located only a few moments from Hyde Park Gardens, a lovely place for strolling.

75_St Mary Magdalene

Art to heal the poor

This church is located on a thin strip of land by the Regent's Canal; the last remaining section of land in the neighbourhood in the 1860s when the church was built. Such was the fervour to lift the spirits of the parish, that little space was not going to be an obstacle. The church was designed by George Edmund Street and finished in 1878.

This was a church built for the poor (to be poor then was to live in a house of three to four families with one tap). A church intended to (quite literally) brighten people's lives with a transformative interior to step into. And to take them out of their grim, miserable existence into colour, splendour, height, texture, gloss, glisten, shine, decoration, lofty arches, a barrel vault and a raised altar to proclaim, yes, there really was a God. And that He could lift you out of your misery, despite your penury and deprivation. The idea behind this was simply to instil reverence in people for whom life provided no hope. It is perhaps no accident then, that the church was dedicated to Mary Magdalene, the ragged haired, bleary-looking, dirty clothed sinner who redeemed herself, with the underlying message that there is hope in faith for us all.

The building was done under the auspices of a Father West, who had been curate of All Saints, Margaret Street. The congregation for services was living nearer Rowington Close and requested a church nearer to home. So, as with all things, we see a contradiction. Who was the real audience who filled up this church on a Sunday morning? If the 'slum rituals' as they were called, were being practised to give hope to the poor, then a blind eye could be turned away from the 'actual' seeing eyes that stared up to God in the church.

Try to see the beautiful chantry chapel below designed by Sir Ninian Comper and look out too for the musical notation along with other painted imagery on the walls.

Address Rowington Close, W2 5TF, +44 (0)207 289 2011, www.st-mary-magdalene.co.uk | **Getting there** Tube to Royal Oak (Hammersmith & City Line), Warwick Avenue (Bakerloo Line); bus: 6, 18, 36, 46, 187 or 414 | **Hours** Mon 9.30–11.30am & 1–3pm, Tue 3–6pm. If you want to visit at another time, please ring or email beforehand to check that it will be possible | **Tip** The church is located right beside the Regent's Canal.

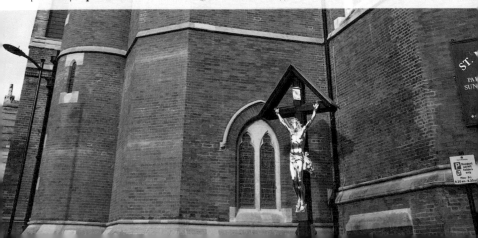

76__St Mary

Its neighbour is the M40

How this adorable church (dating from 1791) has survived to this day is anyone's guess. It is the most immediate neighbour to the M40. A visit might make you believe in miracles, for planners saved this miniature historic building when they built webs of roads, housing estates and a college all around. Nearby is a canal and the church site, possessing many ancient tombs, with faded inscriptions.

The church's façade, facing west, looks partly like a classical temple with a pediment in miniature and has a smart lantern on top. The columned portico is repeated in the east end's apse, except the portico is constructed in the round to mirror the shape of the apse. The church's architecture juxtaposes angularity and circular forms in the most effortless way. There is a very prominent and proud sign above the door in beautiful lettering saying, *Saint Mary's Church on Paddington Green*. One of the reasons the building is so attractive is because it is made of brick with white stone dressings. And its size is most appealing, for it was designed in the shape of a Greek cross, giving a lovely completeness to the space.

Most importantly, the metaphysical poet John Donne preached his first sermon here, but in the church's original state and location dated to 1615. And then William Hogarth (1697–1764), the social satirist in paint, secretly married Jane Thornhill here in 1729. This is also the burial site (on the green, a bit further north) for the infamous actress Sarah Siddons (1755–1831), who transformed herself from lady's maid to celebrity. Look out for the wrought iron cage that encases the tomb and indeed the statue to her. Seated on a high plinth, she is the epitome of the stone muse.

The green itself was once wasteland, but developed after the 18th century and became a space for itinerant selling. Records show that in 1861 a pedlar had set up a stall, 'to expose offensive anatomical drawings'.

Address St Mary's Square, Paddington Green, W2 1LG, +44 (0)207 723 1968,
www.parishoflittlevenice.com | Getting there Mainline to Paddington (Great Western
Railway); Tube to Edgware Road (Bakerloo, Circle and District Lines), Paddington (Circle,
District and Hammersmith & City Lines); bus: 16, 18, 98 or 414 | Hours Sun, Tue and
Thu morning for services | Tip From the church it is only a 15-minute walk to the Lisson
Gallery, dedicated to contemporary art (www.lissongallery.com).

77 __ St Barnabas

Is this really in London?

St Barnabas (meaning son of encouragement) was a missionary travelling in Asia Minor with St Paul, although he was later martyred in 61CE. There is a statue of Barnabas in the church courtyard. The entrance to the church from the street is gated and adds to the rather special feel of the place. The chancel is also brass gated, where you will note a rich display of materials adorning a Sacrament House by the architect Sir Ninian Comper (see ch. 1). He was also married in the church.

The church dates to 1850 and is seen as one of the London churches responding to the reinvigoration of the Catholic faith. It was built by Thomas Cundy junior (1790–1867), who was also the architect of St Gabriel's (see ch. 78). Bringing Popery to Pimlico was considered quite an outrage at the time and the beautiful mosaics on the nave wall, probably done by a family of Italian mosaicists, were considered far too Catholic. Luckily for us, there was no destruction of this Catholic imagery thereafter. It should be better known that some of the wonderful fabric of London churches was made by immigrant artists.

Of note is the mosaic of the *Last Supper*. The figures are placed seated beside a sparsely laid table. We see Judas on the other side of Christ who is standing up and blessing with his right hand. His left hand holds a rather large wafer that looks like a rice cake. Judas is seated, but looking in the direction of the viewer; his head leaning on his hand, his left hand greedily clasping the money bag. Look closer and you will see a sinister expression, in keeping with the stereotypical way in which he is often depicted. The upper room is set against a classically inspired colonnade of arches framing a gold background interlaced with bushes, and reminiscent of many Italian Renaissance paintings. The mosaic is inscribed in memory of Elizabeth Biddulph and dated to 1882.

Address St Barnabas Street, SW1W 8PF, +44 (0)7746 142 457, www.stbarnabaspimlico.com | **Getting there** Tube to Sloane Square (Circle and District Lines), Victoria (Circle, District and Victoria Lines); bus: 11, 44, 170 or 211 | **Hours** Sat 10am–6pm, Sun am, Wed lunchtime for Low Mass | **Tip** Not far from here is the Saatchi gallery (www.saatchigallery.com). And the church is quite close to the River Thames.

78__St Gabriel

Churches at the heart of residential squares

At St Gabriel's, in the middle of Warwick Square, there are roses growing in the church garden, purple flowers creeping through the crevices of the wall bordering the church with the pavement and plants coiling up through iron railings on those nice white houses all around. If you don't manage to find the church open, you can at least admire this pretty patch of nature, and the main front church door allows you to see a small *prie-dieu*, for those on the threshold, as the door opens onto a glass door through which you can see inside.

Church open or closed, you can still sense how, in the middle of so many residential squares in London, churches were at the centre of people's lives. When it was built, the land around was owned by the Marquis of Westminster, who gave £5,000 to land at the south-western end of Warwick Square for a church. The architect was Thomas Cundy junior (1790–1867), the Surveyor of the Grosvenor Estates, and the church was consecrated in 1853. Cundy worked on many of the beautiful residential estates of London, such as Belgravia, giving a harmony of design to this part of west London.

If the stone looks a bit grey and drab to you, that is because it is Kentish ragstone, which unfortunately does not weather well. Inside, of special note, is the east window in the Lady Chapel, with the stained glass of *Christ in Glory*, the design of Charles Eamer Kempe (1837–1907), for whom credit is given to over 400 windows, including work in Turkey and South Africa and places closer to home such as Queens' College, Cambridge. Having spent most of his life working on a large scale, he later moved to Australia where he started to design bookplates.

There is a blue plaque opposite the entrance to the door to the infamous late-Victorian artist Aubrey Beardsley who lived in the house here at 114 Cambridge Street with his mother and sister.

Address Warwick Square, SW1V 2AD, +44 (0)207 834 7520, www.stgabrielspimlico.com |
Getting there Mainline to Victoria (South Western); Tube to Victoria (Circle, District and
Victoria Lines), Pimlico (Victoria Line); bus: 24, 360 or C10 | Hours Sun for 10.30am mass
and then sung evensong and benediction from 6pm. Also sung evensong on Wed at 5pm |
Tip You can visit all the Pimlico churches together in one visit. A 20-minute walk will take
you to Tate Britain.

79___All Saints

A big classical beast of the east

An imposing church in a geographical no man's land, majestic by one curve of the River Thames. When built, the church straddled populous areas where land and water collisions cradled themselves against post-industrial neglect – the Basin of Limehouse, the creeks of Bow, the wharves and buoys, docks and piers around the pit of the Thames; near to where routes north and south, and west and east are fast and furious, and ugly and polluted. Here, mills would have churned, and pushed and spewed out water when London was surging out the full vigorous force of the Industrial Revolution. And now surrounded by Baptist chapels, public baths and a Bible Book museum we can see the great imposing building of All Saints.

It is constructed in an exaggeratedly large classical style, built to the tune of what had become the fashionable style in 18th-century London. It is complete with columns topped by Ionic capitals, bulbous semi-domes sitting within blind arches and portals, apsidal porches and ends, topped up apertures and rising structures and steeples piercing the eye with their corners, projections, turns and smooth faces. Catch the gentle glinting spring light on the building and you might believe you are gazing at ivory. The bulk of the structure though, is such that ivory would be far too costly, as would marble.

All Saints stands like a slowly passing cruise ship on gently moving water, where the windows look like portholes. Despite its mighty structure, the building stands rather forlorn beside the troubled waters and roads of an area of the city where cars exude pollution and fumes and smog as they speed up, slow down, pouring forth angst, energy, music beats and heartbeat. And where the DLR, on its narrow trackway has trains on it that look ready to tumble. Still, we know these buildings can survive the odds. All Saints was built in 1821–23 in order to give the newly forming Poplar parish a place to worship. And still it stands.

Address Newby Place, E14 OEY, +44 (0)207 538 9198, www.parishofpoplar.com | Getting there DLR to All Saints; bus: D8 | Hours Mon–Fri noon–2pm | Tip The Museum of London Docklands is relatively close (www.museumoflondon.org.uk).

80 — St Mary
Debating democracy

This church, with its squat tower, is situated right beside the River Thames. Whether you approach it from the south or the north, it looks like any rural parish church, but don't be fooled by its humble appearance, for this was the location of the Putney Debates of 1647 when, having defeated the monarchy during the English Civil War, the New Model Army met in the church to discuss the role they should play in people's lives. Almost immediately, newly emerging democratic voices began to disagree: Cromwell feared that giving too much power to the people could lead to anarchy, but the Levellers (populists who wanted to level out class distinctions), said that the people are sovereign and that Parliament should be instructed by the people. This was not quite what Cromwell and his elite cronies had in mind. But this conflict echoes today as democracy and what it means is being questioned. Suffrage was also on the agenda, and it was argued that those who were not of property or landowning status should be able to vote. The debates were not resolved at the time, but even so, this understated setting for crucial talks about Parliament and the people, carefully recorded by a scribe, has real historical gravitas. The church now has a comprehensive museum that tells you more about this fascinating period in Britain's history.

Of interest visually is the chantry chapel built in 1513–30 by Bishop Nicholas West who had been baptised in the church. Organising the construction and adornment of a chapel in one's name gave those who could an opportunity to make their mark to ensure their posterity. And the decoration here suggests that he was keen to be remembered.

Samuel Pepys mentions the church in his *Diaries* and at a sermon he 'saw the girls of the schools, few of which pretty'. It doesn't sound like he paid much attention to sermon or prayer!

Address Putney High Street, SW15 1SN, +44 (0)203 903 4732, www.stmarys.parishofputney.com | Getting there Mainline to Putney (South Western); Tube to Putney Bridge (District Line); bus: 14, 39, 74, 85, 93, 220, 270, 424 or 430 | Hours Daily 9am–6pm | Tip You enter the church through the Putney Pantry, so tea or coffee can be drunk before or after the visit.

81 Petersham Parish Church
Visited by Van Gogh

The artist Van Gogh had good taste. We know that he visited Petersham and he may even have visited this perfect, cube-like 18th-century interior of a church. He made a delightful sketch of the Turnham Green congregational chapel and the Petersham Methodist chapel for his brother Theo. In a letter dated 25 November, 1876, he wrote, 'We are pilgrims in the earth and strangers; we come from afar and we are going far'. During this year, he was helping with the poor and sick in Isleworth, not far from Petersham, and he was also later to preach at Petersham Methodist church. No doubt he would have admired the church's location – by meadows near the river.

The church has Norman foundations, and in the early 16th century just about all the church was rebuilt, with further additions made in c. 1600. And then later, in the 17th century, the church's transepts were added, as well as the tower, and later a gallery, which adds to the charm of the interior.

Look at a memorial to Captain George Vancouver (1757–98), the explorer who discovered Vancouver Island, now a haven of celebrities as well as lone wolves. He is buried in the churchyard here. There is also the tomb of the son of Gilbert George Scott who lived nearby. For Gilbert's son John had also redesigned the chancel area of the church in 1874. You might also look out for the grave of Mary Burdekin (d. 1772), who had a pastry shop in Richmond and who is credited as the inventor of the original Maids of Honour cakes which you can still eat at a tea shop by Kew Gardens.

While the church is delightful, go too for the setting of the church, which is located down a dusty path, leading off from a very busy main road. And then not far from the church another path takes you through some gates to Petersham Meadows where cows graze and from where you can walk to the River Thames.

Address Petersham Road, TW10 7AB, +44 (0)208 940 8435, www.southwark.anglican.org | Getting there Mainline to North Sheen (South Western); Tube or Overground to Richmond (District Line), walk through Petersham Meadows from Richmond town centre; bus: 65 or 371 | Hours Thu 10.30–11.30am; Easter to Michaelmas, Sun 3–5pm; Café Sat 10–11am | Tip Ensure that you have time to walk through the meadows to the church, walk by the Thames and then visit some of the many attractive bars and pubs on the Richmond riverside.

82 Holy Trinity
Cholera in London and piled up bodies

Here is a church, graveyard, city farm with animals and a vegetable plot, and water and skyscrapers on the horizon all visible on this pocket of land by the River Thames. As Dickens recalls in *Our Mutual Friend*, the area embodies the great, exhilarating diversity found with people – he writes of Eugene Wrayburn finding humanity washed from higher ground and taken down by sewage. This is an area where we might think of the relationship between bodies and water. During the 19th century, cholera, especially for the poor, was deadly. Dead bodies were piled one on top of the other. Given the proximity of the graveyard to the water at the Thames, the bodies were a sort of filter for the water as it drained down and then moved back upwards. As this caused dreadful choleric outbreaks, the church had to close. In the graveyard here is the headstone of what must have been a pauper's grave, as it was made of wood.

On a cheerier note, the purpose-built Victorian church originally housed 1,500 people. They got the faith bad in those days, perhaps not surprisingly. The church was bombed in a 7 September, 1940 blitz raid. There is a photograph of the bombed-out church with its 19th-century Gothic arch at the chancel end. How different from how it looks now. There is a tiny Crucifix in a glass case that was found in the ruins of the damaged church, which was saved by a parishioner.

The church is now cool and bright 1950s territory. And so, the great 20th-century muralist Hans Feibusch painted the subject of *Christ on the Cross* (1960), which has a particularly lovely rendition of Jerusalem in the background. Now it has weathered, it looks a little less modernist than it would have done originally. Those less keen on modernism detested the work, which is somewhat ironic when a major influence on Feibusch was Italian Renaissance fresco painting.

Address 3 Bryan Road, SE16 5HF, +44 (0)7948 806 809, www.holy-trinity-rotherhithe.org.uk | **Getting there** Tube or Overground to Canada Water (Jubilee Line); bus: C10 or 381; river boat: Greenland Pier (Thames Clippers), Nelson Dock Pier (Canary Wharf Ferry) | **Hours** One Sat every month, Sun and Thu am for a service | **Tip** The large Mudchute Park and Farm are nearby, right on the river, and from there you can walk along the river in either direction.

83__St Mary
A Turner connection

One of the most beautiful churches and settings, and very close to the River Thames, St Mary's rebuilt (1716) church, according to the design of John James, closely connected to Sir Christopher Wren and with later additions by William Butterfield (1876). The parishioners, mainly seamen and watermen, had to pay for a lot of this themselves. There are cobbled streets, old pubs and points of interest at the river a stone's throw away.

The word 'Rotherhithe' may have stemmed from two Saxon words – *redhra* or *rothra* meaning 'mariner' and *hyth* meaning 'haven.' There are many wharves in this area, recalling its past as an important maritime area. It is also important, as in 1620 the *Mayflower* launched from Rotherhithe with the Pilgrim Fathers on its epic journey to America. It was captained by Christopher Jones, a Rotherhithe resident.

One of Turner's most famous paintings is *The Fighting Temeraire Tugged to her Last Berth to be Broken Up* (1839). In the church, note two Bishops' chairs, made from timber from the actual ship, a gun ship that had been used at the Battle of Trafalgar (1805). The ship was dismantled in 1838. That same year, Turner was in a boat with friends and they saw the ship being towed to the breaker's yard. They must have known what it was, and so Turner duly recorded its poignant end in paint. He takes a historical subject for eulogy, but also for elegy, and renders it into something that breaks the conventions of painting where form and line, volume and shape have absolute clarity. But for Turner, a lack of form can still capture a ship being moved slowly up the Thames. And so, we see how even chairs carry the enormous weight of history.

Visit late afternoon in summer and you will find an atmospheric quality that seems to have come from nowhere. The church spire is tall and gracious, as is the layout of the church, as is the church information leaflet, measuring some 45 centimetres (18 inches).

Address Marychurch Street, SE16 4JE, +44 (0)207 394 3394, www.stmaryrotherhithe.org | Getting there Overground to Canada Water and Rotherhithe; Tube to Bermondsey or Canada Water (Jubilee Line); bus: 47, 188, 381 or C10 | Hours On days when services are advertised (see website) | Tip The Brunel Museum is nearby, where you can visit the Engine House (www.brunel-museum.org.uk) and, on weekend evenings, enjoy a drink in the Midnight Apothecary garden.

84__St Paul
Acoustics of the highest order

The partly 18th-century church is situated on the 'Highway'. The church was rebuilt in 1820, but dates to 1656 when it was originally built as a chapel of ease to St Dunstan, Stepney (see ch. 94). Imagine carts chasing into London town, with the danger of kidnap and ransom, hijack and robbery during this period. Or the slow-moving respectful hearse accompanied by black-coated figures and ladies draped in black lace we might associate with the 19th century. The building is majestic, tall and wide. There is a garden all around, gravestones are banked up against the wall and trees are silent in the still air. In her biography of Charlotte Brontë, Mrs Gaskell refers to people in clogs in churches who make such a noise as they 'cluttered and clumped' around the church. But not here, as this is little visited. Absorb the silence. But then, also the music.

This is a considerably vast space, with a stage with music-making equipment: the music is for the service, as this is called a 'modern' church. The acoustics are quite something. You might visit churches with bigger domes, but stand underneath this one and listen to how your voice echoes and resonates as if it is magnified by the sound system of the stage. But it is not. You, alone, can create acoustic heaven here.

Outside, the red noticeboard lists some famous people. Thomas Jefferson's mother was baptised here, as was Walter Pater (1839–94), the great Victorian writer and art critic, and John Wesley preached here.

It is said that over 75 ships' captains are buried in the churchyard, as Shadwell is near to the Thames and gained a reputation as a nautical church. Unusually, J. Walters, the architect, is commemorated in stone on the façade and on the other side of the doorway, even more unusually, see the inscription to R. Streather, the builder. He made an edifice of height and elegance, eloquence and majesty.

Address The Highway, Tower Hamlets, E1W 3DI1, +44 (0)207 680 2772, www.sps.church | Getting there Overground or DLR to Shadwell; bus: 15 or 100 | Hours During service times; check website | Tip Afterwards you can walk to The Shadwell Basin Outdoor Activity Centre, a great place for water sports and all manner of adventurous activities (www.shadwell-basin.co.uk).

85 All Saints

The mural painting of Hans Feibusch

At the high altar of this light and bright modern church is a mural by Hans Feibusch (a prolific mural painter of religious subjects who is not that well known). He was a Jewish-German refugee who came to England in the 1930s. He later converted to Christianity, but towards the end of his life returned to Judaism. Before his arrival in England, he had worked in Frankfurt and was chosen by Hitler and Goebbels as one of the artists to represent the 'degenerate art' associated with Modernism in Munich in 1937. He is principally known as a mural painter for many a church altar, and wrote a book on mural painting.

The mural depicts the *Ascension of Christ* and was painted soon after the church was built in the 1950s. The work is on a large scale and the emphasis is on the drama: the bodies are gestural and emotional as they react to the moment when Christ ascends. He is central and surrounded by angels in pink and ochre, giving a spring-like feel to an otherwise cold and airy church. The Apostles stand on the ground, all flesh and muscle, in a range of positions. One is even crouched in the crook of a tree, hands as if about to pray with head bent; is this the demeanour of disbelief? Feibusch also inverts precedent pictorial traditions, as instead of painting the stronger colours at the centre to draw the eye, the colours become stronger as they radiate outwards, as if to remind the viewer to look at the whole work, and not just at Christ. Despite the limitations of the fresco technique where there is only scope for a light wash before the plaster dries, the artist paints bodies and landscape in a bold and vigorous way with seemingly so few brushstrokes. Fresco can have real visual power.

Feibusch was a brave, radical, and authentic artist – a breath of fresh air in the 1950s. All Saints is one of several churches in London where you can see his murals.

Address Herbert Road, Woolwich, SE18 3PU, +44 (0)208 854 2995,
www.allsaintsshootershill.org/index.html | Getting there Mainline to Woolwich Arsenal
(Southeastern); DLR to Woolwich Arsenal; bus: 386 stops right outside | Hours
Fri 10–11am or Sun when the church is open for services | Tip While you are in the area,
you can visit another Feibusch church in Eltham (St Barnabas) or Welling (St Mary the
Virgin) and the Woolwich Garrison church built in the 19th century to serve the Woolwich
artillery, with its splendid mosaics (see ch. 111).

86__Holy Trinity
William Morris-like aesthetic

Built from 1888 by John Dando Sedding, brother and pupil of George Edmund Street (see ch. 56), this church brought back a belief in the importance of craft. Sedding, like John Ruskin and William Morris, was an apostle of the Arts and Crafts movement – loving the pure, authentic, rough shapes of nature, which they felt could be brought inside into buildings such as churches. On the whole, these were men born into wealth who saw industrialism encroaching and wanted to remind themselves of the light, the shade, the texture, the scroll, the foliage, the petal, rush and reed, of natural forms that so many were leaving behind as they trod towards London, Manchester and Birmingham to find work.

You will not miss the church, but if you think you might, look out for the bikes waiting for your ride thanks to Santander. Or look for some graceful lettering: *this corner stone of ye church of the holy trinity erected by George 5th Earl Cadogan as laid by Beatrix Countess Cadogan on Ascension Day May 30, 1889.* And a little inscription below saying *J. D. Sedding, Arch.*, to commemorate the architect. Inside, we also see his profile portrait on a memorial where two angels kneel. The monument was made by the Art Workers' Guild. It seems to be a playful take on angels not protecting and supporting holy figures, but the maker and creator of this audaciously decorated church. But of course, it was the Cadogan family, clearly of immense wealth, who could afford such lavish ornamentation. They could even afford to get Pre-Raphaelite artists along such as Edward Burne-Jones (1833–98) and Morris to design stained glass for the church.

See the beautiful embroidery by Sedding's wife, Rose, on the memorial to Sedding, consisting of lovingly threaded thistles with a deer whose antlers are as sharp and thorny as the thistles curling up above the creature.

Address Sloane Street, SW1X 9BZ, +44 (0)207 730 7270, www.sloanechurch.org | **Getting there** Tube to Sloane Square (Circle and District Lines); bus: 11, 19, 211 or 360 | **Hours** Daily, normal office hours | **Tip** This is a very smart address – for shopping in Sloane Street and King's Road.

87 __ St Patrick

Visit Soho, see Venice

The church is in an area once notorious for its slums and gin drinking. Following the *Catholic Relief Acts* of 1778 and 1791, it was built for Irish immigrants living in the area. The Acts gave Catholics more freedom to worship than had been granted to them since the Reformation. The current church dates to c. 1893; the architect was John Kelly (1840–1904).

The interior contains the most stunning apse. You might imagine you are in Torcello Cathedral or St Mark's Basilica in Venice. The effect is a glorious, gold, painted and bold space. The interior is high, mighty and white, clean and bright. The columns are large and creamy, with elaborate capitals in the classical style.

The church is full of people coming and going, to watch and wonder, or pray. It also organises lots of events: a Pilgrimage to Rome, the Stations of the Cross ceremony every Friday before Lent, Vigil Mass for St Patrick on his special day of 16 March, an opening 24 hours for the Day for the Lord, a request by Pope Francis that each diocese in the world has one church open for 24 hours for Eucharist, and priests available for confession throughout the night. St Patrick's is also one large, friendly open house serving London's poor and homeless in London and anybody else who wants to feel part of something in the centre of the capital.

That sense of belonging is felt, too, in an altarpiece dedicated to Martha and Mary (Magdalen). You might see them in a side panel or a *predella*, at the base of an altarpiece, but not usually as central figures. Martha and Mary are sisters. Martha keeps house, while Mary contemplates; Martha wishing her sister would be less idle. They were also the sisters of Lazarus, whom Christ brings back from the dead. Of course, when Mary Magdalen is placed beside Jesus, her reputation concerns her sinning humanity and she is altogether more interesting.

Address 21a Soho Square, W1D 4NR, +44 (0)207 437 2010, www.parish.rcdow.org.uk |
Getting there Tube or Crossrail to Tottenham Court Road (Central and Northern Lines);
bus: 1, 14, 24, 38, 94, 98 or 176 | **Hours** Daily, all day | **Tip** The church is right in the heart
of Soho. Enough said.

88_ St Stephen
A woodland church

A church situated in an exclusive, leafy, residential area of South London. And what a place for peace, trees and art. St Stephen's was the setting for a painting called *Sydenham Hill* (1870) by the Impressionist, Camille Pissarro (1830–1903), who painted scenes of London when he was living for a while in nearby Lower Norwood.

Go through the tollgate (walking is free, but cars pay) and see the well-established trees of Sydenham Woods, looking up to Crystal Palace. With the tall spire ahead, this is the view that Pissarro captures in his painting. And because the road is a quiet one, it does not look dissimilar today.

The church, designed by Charles Barry junior (1823–1900), the son of Charles Barry who designed the Houses of Parliament, has a plain Victorian exterior, flanked by foliage and box hedges. Inside is a blue star-spangled chancel ceiling; in the nave, a floral decorated ceiling, with pillars bordered by white plastered angels.

Of especial note is the Edward Poynter (1836–1919) fresco in the chancel (1871–73) dedicated to St Stephen, the Christian martyr stoned to death and painted in the idiom of Italian Renaissance fresco painting. It is rare to see a fresco intact in Britain. Stephen looks like a 'blond angel', the preferred 'look' in Christian art. He is also quite feminine looking, despite the strength needed to combat evil forces. His deacon's robe is decorated with little crowns; a play on his name – *Stephanos*, Greek for 'crown.' Look for his stoning by the mob and the officious Roman soldiers pushing him along, following his announcement that he had seen 'the son of Man, sitting at the right hand of God'.

To the left of the fresco is his cartoon (drawing) as preparation for the fresco, which you could study to see if he made any changes along the way. Poynter was director of the National Gallery and Painter at the Houses of Parliament.

Address College Road, Dulwich, SE21 7HW, +44 (0)208 693 3797, www.ststephensdulwich.org | **Getting there** Mainline to Sydenham Hill (Southeastern), West Dulwich (Southeastern); bus: 3, 303 or 450 | **Hours** Tue 8–10am, Wed 8am–5pm, Thu 8–9.30am, Fri 8am–noon, Sat 10.30–11.30am, Sun 7.30am–12.30pm | **Tip** Close by are Sydenham Woods and a short walk from here is the Dulwich Picture Gallery.

89__St Augustine
Virginia Woolf and churches

The church of St Augustine was established out of a garden shed. In 1865, the Reverend R. R. Chope put up a church in his garden, until it was decided a more suitable church should take its place. William Butterfield (1814–1900), one of the legendary late-Victorian architects, was commissioned to build the church in 1865.

Inside are lots of materials: red brick, yellow and blue slate and marble, mosaics and pigments for the murals, customary for many late-Victorian churches. This 'look', though, went out of fashion in the 1920s with white washing, but the building's original layer was uncovered again in the 1970s.

Virginia Woolf grew up nearby in Hyde Park Gate. In her novel, *Mrs Dalloway* (1925), Elizabeth observes the street life around Temple, noting the river and the church. Yet, although she was a great observer of people, places and things, and even though many of Woolf's novels were set in London, churches are not often referred to. If she had frequented the churches in Kensington, St Augustine might have been one of them. It is still a working church, but also a community hub, and one can only imagine her observing the people coming and going, having their hair cut, chatting with a cup of coffee or commenting perhaps on their having a safe place and a sense of belonging. We know that she liked watching people in Kensington Gardens: old ladies in hats, people walking, children with their hoops or sticks, and people gazing and talking. It is interesting, then, that she did not think to spend much time in a church people watching, as no doubt there would have been plenty to divert her. As a lover of history, though, she would have learned that in the 18th century, there was a workhouse for the poor not far from her house in Kensington Gate and then one at St Mary Abbots (see ch. 58). The community hub at St Augustine fits well into that historical legacy.

Address 115a Queen's Gate, SW7 5LP, +44 (0)845 644 7533, www.achurchnearyou.com |
Getting there Tube to South Kensington (Circle, District and Piccadilly Lines); bus: 49,
70, 74 or 345 | **Hours** Contact church prior to any visit | **Tip** Nearby is the Albert Hall and
Kensington Gardens where Virginia Woolf and her sister Vanessa Bell used to walk when
they were living as children at Hyde Park Gate. There is a blue plaque in Hyde Park Gate
marking the house where Woolf grew up.

90 All-Hallows-the-Great

Treasures all bricked up

Look for a tranquil corner at the junction of Copperfield Street and Pepper Street, south of Southwark Street and directly south of Tate Modern. On Copperfield Street, the post-war residents of the area had a parish church, the church of All Hallows, a splendid example of Victorian Gothic architecture, designed by Gilbert George Scott junior (c. 1879). Now it is slightly dwarfed by higher buildings all round.

This is also the hidden bricked up world of Hans Feibusch. From Goring-by-Sea to Welling and Rotherhithe, this artist was also in Southwark. There is a mural by him in this walled up church. The painter, whose art gets right to the stomach, hits you with his figures, all flesh, but without having to be thickly painted body and cloth. It is a gift that is hard to pinpoint, as is the sense of place here, which you might see when you wander the back streets, alleyways, paths, courtyards, arches and overgrown gardens of this little area of London. It represents the remnants of a tiny part of SE1 that was not bombed in World War II.

Once long ago, this area was also the denizen of bear pits, raucous plays, prisons and brothels. Now it is a very central area of London, and now, too, a major centre for high-tech modern regeneration in the form of old warehouses, studios and churches which are now architects' offices and the ubiquitous tower block, making the identification of the differentiation of suburbs and areas of London harder.

The back of the church, today a little torn asunder, now with ivy and growth filling in bricked in arches is the backdrop. You can sit down and imagine how the church used to be and admire a row of pristine Victorian cottages, called Winchester Cottages. The Winchester geese were prostitutes that we know the medieval Bishop of Winchester licensed and assumedly also enjoyed.

Address Copperfield Street, SE1 0EP, www.cathedral.southwark.anglican.org | Getting
there Tube to Blackfriars (Circle and District Lines), Southwark (Jubilee Line), London
Bridge (Jubilee and Northern Lines); bus: 344 | Hours Accessible 24 hours (exterior only) |
Tip The church is about 14 minutes' walk from the food market at Borough and The Old
Operating Theatre Museum (www.oldoperatingtheatre.com).

91__Christchurch
Civic imagery in a church

To see a church that has civic imagery in it as well as religious art is a rare thing. But this rather cutting-edge, modernist space (we are in a rebuilt post-1945 London Blitz church, dating from 1961), is a testament to the history of Southwark as well as to Christianity.

On small windows to the right of the church, as you enter, you will see small stained glass roundels of various Southwark scenes. Look out for the picture of Sainsbury's, complete with a laden shopping trolley being led by a mother and child; another scene is dedicated to other lively images of Southwark's history and organisations connected with it, buildings and people.

Higher up to the right and left with your back to the altar, are scenes celebrating Southwark's industries done by Kenneth Bunton in 1959. There are men heaving sacks, a view of a printing machine and workers and two men working in a baker's shop with lots of loaves laid out. There is also a delightful scene of three women waiting for a red London bus. One of them waits with her shopping bag revealing a couple of fish, which she must have just bought at market. Some of the scenes also have beautiful lettering on them such as *Unity is Strength* on the window for 14 trade union branches.

The altar space where you would expect to find Christian imagery has a large gold coloured cross attached to a massive blown up black and white photograph of rooftops and towers, which is presumably another reference to Southwark and the church's location just to the south of Blackfriars Bridge.

Behind the church is a small garden where you can sit and admire the architecture, or look towards the high-rises that now border the River Thames. When the church was originally built, dating back to 1631, there was no Blackfriars Bridge here. It was bequeathed by a 'whitebaker' called John Marshall, who must have done rather well in this trade.

Address 27 Blackfriars Road, SE1 8NY, +44 (0)207 205 4707, www.christchurchsouthwark.org.uk | Getting there Mainline to Blackfriars (Thameslink), London Bridge (Thameslink, South Western and Southeastern); Tube to London Bridge (Jubilee and Northern Lines), Blackfriars (Circle and District Lines); bus: 40, 63, 139, 211 or 381 | Hours Mon–Sat 9am–6pm, Sun 10am–6pm | Tip You can walk over Blackfriars Bridge towards Smithfield and the City.

92 __ St George's Cathedral

A London cathedral, but without the crowds

A little-visited church space, and yet it is one of the cathedrals of London.

Augustus Pugin (1812–52) designed and built the cathedral in 1841–48, although the current space dates from 1953. He wanted to revive Gothic art and architecture into a London fabric that had been transformed by the 18th-century classical style. Look at the Palace of Westminster as an example of what sort of look Pugin wanted to create for a nation where industrialisation and population growth had brought about what he saw as a curse on faith and architecture. For him, the Gothic style was characteristically British, and he wanted people to feel something that had been lost, born again. He advocated spires, heights, pointed arches, statues in niches, sculptural encyclopaedias, tracery, colour, lofty views, and the sort of mood and ritual that had not been seen in England since before the 18th century. Pugin rejected the cool calculations of the geometry and ratios of classical architecture. He saw Catholicism as synonymous with the Gothic style, while Protestantism signalled the classical, and pagan. He also felt that church spaces should inhabit the grace of the old, rather than the perils of the new, which was mass machine produced work. For Pugin, people would be happier if religion was returned to the fold. Whether his point on decay of religion and style resonated with the popular imagination then is a moot point, as so much was defaced at the time of the Reformation, so would people have understood what he meant?

The remains of the blackened sleeping figures on the altar fragment by Pugin are a crucial and poignant remnant of St George's before the massive bomb that hit it in 1941. Other poignant Gothic fragments include the Blessed Sacrament Chapel, which has survived from his building campaign.

Pugin had redesigned 30 churches by the time he was 30, as well as 3 cathedrals.

Address Lambeth Road, Southwark, SE1 6HR, +44 (0)207 928 5256,
www.stgeorgescathedral.org.uk | Getting there Mainline to Waterloo (Southeastern
and South Western); Tube to Waterloo (Waterloo & City, Jubilee and Northern Lines),
Lambeth North and Elephant and Castle (Bakerloo Line); bus: 12, 148, 155, 344 or 363 |
Hours Mon–Fri 7am–6pm, Sat 9am–7pm, Sun 7.30am–7pm | Tip Not far away is the
Tibetan Peace Garden and the Imperial War Museum, which has a World War II gallery
and a café (www.iwm.org.uk).

93___St Mark

A church of grandeur for grandiose living

A magnificent church in a magnificent street and with a magnificent interior which you might have all to yourself. An austere grey stone exterior, with little additional moulding; but step inside to a vast space and imagine how, in the mid-19th century, the church was built large to accommodate the need for about 1,500 people. Perhaps this is where Lewis Carroll worshipped, as he lived close by at 5 Abbey Road.

The Victorians' approach to medievalising is seen in many decorative details: William Morris-like embroidery curtains to draw across a pointed arched doorway, the grooved and folded lines of panelling on a wooden seat, the highly polished wooden floor tiles and a colourful Victorian aesthetic, such as the mosaics of religious figures with dedications to local women of the late 19th century. This is a vast structure of beams and rafters, wooden balconies and pews, as if it were a ship to be launched to a far-flung Empire destination. The church embodies a confidence associated with the Victorian spirit of endeavour.

In the chapel of St Stephen and St George at the end of the north aisle is a mural (1952) by Sigismund Christian Hubert Goetze to the memory of World War I soldiers and nurses. Here is *St Michael Defeating the Dragon*, with a naval figure and a soldier holding British flags, a man in RAF uniform, and a nurse in clean white and blue uniform, with head-dress, kneeling and praying. Above is an image of *Christ in Glory* surrounded by angels. Artwork evoking patriotism wrought by the ravages of war and enshrined in the triumphant zeal of Christian militarism. The picture aims to be heroic and instils the value of looking up to a resplendent Christ who helped win the war. Such splendour could reinstate a nation's sense of survival. To think this was painted only a short while after people in parlours were arguing over the merits of a Creator God.

Address 114 Hamilton Terrace, St John's Wood, NW8 9UT, +44 (0)20 7624 4065, www.stmarks.london | Getting there Tube to Maida Vale (Bakerloo Line), St John's Wood (Jubilee Line); bus: 16, 98, 139, 316 or 332 | Hours Please call the Administrator to enquire about bookings, though the church can be open in the day and on Sun | Tip The church is in the same street as a blue plaque to Joseph William Bazalgette (1819–91) the visionary Victorian civil engineer who created London's sewage system. It is worth visiting his stunning Crossness Pumping Station for more glorious Victorian design.

94_ St Dunstan and All Saints

Like an ancient village church

If you go down to the East End one day, you might be surprised by how green and rural it can be. This charming Kentish ragstone structure could be the village parish church, surrounded as it is by ancient stones and graves in the churchyard stretching out before you.

The church has an ancient pedigree. A wooden structure was rebuilt in the 10th century by Dunstan (d. 988, canonised 1029), a talented man, who was not only the Bishop of London, but also the Lord of the Manor of Stepney, and eventually a saint! In 960 he became Archbishop of Canterbury. He was advisor to many English kings and his Coronation service is still used. He was a scholar, but also musician, metalworker and bell founder. Indeed, the bells here are recorded in the famous nursery rhyme – 'Oranges and Lemons say the bells of St Clement's… when will that be, say the bells of Stepney'. Images of St Dunstan show him in his forge while the Devil tempts him, so Dunstan burns his nose with his hot tongs and swiftly banishes him. You can see a small relief carving of the Devil and tongs over the entrance to the church.

You can also still see something of the pre-10th-century church foundation with a Saxon stone rood by the east window. In the south aisle is the original staircase that leads to the rood screen. The church also contains a rare 14th-century relief of the *Annunciation*.

Now, despite the urban encroachment it faces on all sides, the strength the stone building conveys looks set to stay.

Outside, there are many graves of sailors, which gives the church the appellation 'Church of the High Seas'. It is situated not far from Ratcliffe, one of the London ports. Many 17th-century plague victims are also buried here. It is also worth looking for the tomb of Sir Henry Colet (d. 1505), who was twice Mayor of London, a friend of Erasmus and Thomas More and who had 22 children.

Address Stepney High Street, E1 0NR, +44 (0)207 702 8685, www.stdunstanstepney.com |
Getting there Tube to Stepney Green (Circle, District and Hammersmith & City Lines;
DLR to Limehouse; bus: 25, 205, 309 or 339 | Hours Tue & Fri 9.30am–5pm, Thu
10am–noon, Sat 10am–4pm | Tip Stepney City Farm is right beside the church.

95__Georgian Orthodox
Animal statues and a love sect

A fascinating area of London where you might see churches on one side of the road, and synagogues on the other. Wander up Stamford Hill, a truly multicultural road, where Jewish hat and clothing shops are in close proximity to trendy concept ware shops and cafés full of people drinking coffee while staring at their laptops. The furthest north and most easterly place to visit is Clapton Common, where you will see a Jewish school, but also a synagogue just off the common and then a completely unexpected wonder. A palatial looking church behind high gates around it and with overblown statues of animals on the turrets to greet you: a man, a lion, an eagle, an ox, the symbols of the Evangelists. And they all have wings, ready to fly away. These were done by Arthur George Walker (a Royal Academician).

The architects were a family concern: Joseph Morris, his daughters Violet and Olive, a woodcarver, and his sons Francis and Henry Silver. They belonged to the Agapemonite sect, although according to the *Daily Telegraph*, the sect was called the Abode of Love, and founded by a defrocked priest alleged to have had sex with a virgin on a billiard table in front of his followers! One J. H. Smyth Piggott claimed he was God and that he could walk on Clapton Pond.

The church (1892–95) exterior looks notably Victorian. Now the interior is notably Georgian Orthodox with the characteristic screen hiding the altar area and a few icons dotted around. But the chief wonder is the brightly coloured stained glass panels by Walter Crane (dated to 1896) (see ch. 99) of flowers and curling plant forms such as rose, lily, vine, fig, olive and iris. This is natural history in a church – there is no traditional religious subject matter in sight, apart from Elijah and Enoch. What you see instead in the glass are basically personifications of themes such as sin, death, disease and shame.

Address Rookwood Street, N16 6SS | **Getting there** Overground to Stamford Hill; bus: 253, 318, 349 or W9 | **Hours** Any reasonable time, but best not to visit on Sun mornings when services are on. You enter via a buzzer if the church doors are not open | **Tip** A fascinating area of synagogues and the church of St Thomas, Clapton Common, built in the classical style, are also worth a look.

96 Newington Green Meeting House

Mary Wollstonecraft connections

This non-religious meeting house, thought to be one of London's oldest places of non-conformist worship, has been associated with political radicalism for over three centuries. Stoke Newington attracted many Dissenters in the 18th century, including the writer and philosopher, Mary Wollstonecraft (1759–97), author of *A Vindication of the Rights of Woman* (1792).

The current 19th-century building is striking with its stuccoed front and pilasters and entablature topped by a pediment. If it were not for the notices outside, it would be easy to mistake it for a residential building.

When Mary Wollstonecraft first set up a school on this Green in 1784, Stoke Newington was a small country suburb near London. There were tall Georgian houses and trees in the Green and this is where Mary first got involved with dissenting religions. If she looked out of the window of her school, she could see this rather elegant chapel. The minister in charge then was Dr Richard Price, who had become renowned for his radical views. He lived on the Green with his wife, in a red brick terrace, dating back to 1658. He communicated with Benjamin Franklin, Thomas Jefferson and Joseph Priestly, another Dissenter, who was of enormous influence also on shaping Wollstonecraft's views. Priestly is also known as the discoverer of oxygen.

Another woman associated with the church and who worshipped here is Anna Laetitia Barbauld (1743–1825) for whom there is a dedication plaque in the church. Her husband, Rochemont Barbauld, was preacher from 1808, but he went mad, and drowned himself in the New River. A plaque inside, *With wit, genius, poetic talent, and a vigorous understanding, she promot(ed) the cause of humanity, peace, and justice, of civil and religious liberty*, suggests a woman of some status at the time.

Address 39a Stoke Newington Green, N16 9PR, +44 (0)207 354 0774, www.new-unity.org/getstarted | Getting there Overground to Canonbury and then 10 minutes' walk; bus: 21, 73, 141, 236, 341 or 476 | Hours Wed–Sat 10am–4pm; book private group tours for Mon & Tue 10–4pm in advance, through NGMH.org.uk | Tip A 15-minute walk will bring you to the atmospheric Abney Park Cemetery just off Stoke Newington Church Street.

97__Old Church

A church built in the Elizabethan period

The Old Church is at the end of Stoke Newington Church Street, a delightful road that curves and bends and meanders, like a river, to the church and the equally charming Clissold Park. The Old Church should not be mistaken for the church of St Mary's, which is on the other side of the road. Here is a woodland like setting, with well-established trees, where the church nestles within, although its spire and brickwork make it stand out. Above the porch at the south entrance a plaque reads *1563 Ab alto*, meaning 'from above'. A wonderfully brief inscription to justify the adage less is more.

When most churches we see in London are layers of buildings often going back to Anglo-Saxon times and were therefore originally Catholic, it is unusual to see a church that although had medieval origins, exists today as a building established during the Protestant reign of Elizabeth I (from 1563). And although the church was badly bombed in World War II, you can still see some of the original brickwork inside.

Like many Dissenters associated with Stoke Newington Green Meeting House, the churchyard has some tombs of people involved in the abolition of slavery. For example, James Stephen's (William Wilberforce's brother-in-law, and involved in the anti-slavery bill) tomb in the south-eastern part of the churchyard. Mary Barbauld, another Dissenter in Wollstonecraft's circle (see ch. 96), is also buried here, although the lettering on the tomb is very hard to make out. And William Wilberforce's sister and daughters' graves can also be found here.

Inside, you will see a mixture of 18th- and 19th-century furnishings, including box pews from the latter period. However, the church is normally only open for events, so it is best to check first before you make a special trip. On a summer's day though the exterior and location can't be beaten.

Address Stoke Newington Church Street, N16 9ES, www.theoldchurch.org.uk |
Getting there Overground to Stoke Newington; Tube to Highbury & Islington (Northern
and Victoria Lines), then a 20-minute walk to Stoke Newington Church Street; bus: 106,
141 or 149 | **Hours** For events, check the website | **Tip** Stoke Newington Church Street is
a delightful street full of quirky individual shops and cafés. It is also located very close to
Abney Park Cemetery.

98 Savoy Chapel
A place of worship for the Queen

The chapel is on the site of John of Gaunt's Savoy Palace. Gaunt was the husband of Blanche, great-granddaughter of Edmund, 1st Earl of Lancaster. So, from the start, the chapel had royal connections. During the 18th century, the chapel was the place to go for an illegal marriage service. But the vicar was arrested and transported. Ironically, in the 19th century, it became fashionable for the upper classes to marry here. Later, divorcees were able to remarry here under the direction of Hugh Boswell Chapman (d. 1933), who himself was vice-president of the Divorce Reform Union. In Evelyn Waugh's novel, *Brideshead Revisited*, Julia, in discussion with her lover, Charles, themselves both divorcees, says of the Savoy, 'the place where divorced couples got married in those days – a poky little place'. From 1890, it became the first place of worship in London to operate with electricity. In 1939, it became a royal chapel. The land here is owned by the Duchy of Lancaster, and the landlady is the Queen.

Note the tiny figurines of women on tall pedestals facing towards the altar. On the left, is Alicia, the daughter of Simon Steward (1579–1629), who was a poet and interested in fairies! He built a monument to his own father and his son Robert in Ely Cathedral, but what is known of Alicia? Note too from her death in 1573 that her father outlived her. On the other side is Nicola Moray, who was the wife of Sir Robert Douglas and accordingly they married at St Mary Woolnoth (see ch. 33). But she died in childbirth. The *Dictionary of National Biography* was not helpful in identifying these women.

There is a museum about the chapel's history and some of the historical figures associated with it. You will also see a drawing by the Pre-Raphaelite artist, Edward Burne-Jones. There are also engravings by the excellent 17th-century engraver, Wenceslaus Hollar of London.

Address Savoy Hill, WC2R 0DA, +44 (0)207 836 7221, www.royalchapelsavoy.org |
Getting there Tube to Temple (Circle and District Lines), Embankment (Circle and
District Lines); bus: 6, 59, 168, 171, 172 or X68 | Hours Mon–Thu 9am–4pm, Sun
9am–1pm (worship only), closed after the first Sunday after Christmas and Easter and
in August and September | Tip Afterwards, you can visit the National Gallery or one of
London's architectural treasures nearby, called Two Temple Place (www.twotempleplace.org).

99__Christchurch
The Star of David

This is a tall, late-Victorian church, close to a busy urban highway, with the Star of David interlocked on the façade. It has the appearance of some of the unadorned Romanesque churches, in tripartite design that you see in locations such as Venice. The church was built for artisans and has the feel of an artisan led church. The façade is constructed of brick for example. Yet, the tower rises to 34 metres (111 feet) and gives the church stature as well.

You will see the screen. This was a way to protect and honour the altar and the space when the priest stands by the altar. The posts are gone, but of course the altar isn't. Before us, behind the altar, is a rich set of stained glass windows with a host of characters from St Francis, to Bishop Ken and John Keble, a protagonist of the Tractarian movement.

There is also an apse containing mosaics, made in the model of Venetian Romanesque designs such as at the 9th-century cathedral of Torcello. These include the *Supper at Emmaus*. Christ stands and looks out. He holds some bread, as if he is blessing. The two guests don't look that amazed that he is with them. Perhaps the moment portrayed here is some time after Christ has announced himself as the Saviour and they are accustomed to his presence. You will also see the *Nativity*, with the Christ child laid out on a trestle table on a bed of straw. Mary kneels, while Joseph stands, holding a staff of some size.

Note the two very Pre-Raphaelite looking windows designed by Walter Crane (1845–1915), the famous late 19th-century book illustrator. See his initials within a little circle in the bottom right. Look at the modern stained glass with the *Crucifixion* to the right in a little chapel as you face the altar. You can just make out the head and shoulders of two figures in brown, partly in profile who are perhaps acting as witnesses to the event.

Address 3 Christchurch Road, SW2 3ET, +44 (0)208 674 5723,
www.christchurchstreatham.org.uk | **Getting there** Mainline to Streatham Hill (Southern),
Tulse Hill (Southern); Tube to Brixton (Victoria Line); bus: 57, 109, 118, 133, 137, 159,
201, 250 or 333 | **Hours** Check for service times on website to enable access | **Tip** Lots of
parks and commons nearby to choose from for green space.

100__ St Leonard
Monuments galore

Like so many churches, this building has layers of architectural history, from Anglo-Saxon foundation to the medieval, the early 19th century to the 1970s when there was a dreadful fire. Enter today through a vestibule (which used to be part of the church), with a classicising monument to John Howland, where cherubs and a skull sit side by side and a Renaissance monument of a man and wife who face one another, called the Massingberd memorial. The church is a treasure trove of historical gems.

There are monuments to the Thrale family, local landowners, who lived in Streatham Park. Some of the family's illustrious 18th-century luminaries are buried in the vault in the crypt. Henry Thrale (1724/9–81) and his wife Hester were close friends of Dr (Samuel) Johnson (1709–84), the legendary essayist and famed for his dictionary. He used to visit the church. Hester Thrale wrote the *Anecdotes of Dr Johnson*, who, incidentally, loved the 14th-century structure of the church (now gone). In the south aisle is what is called a 'mourning tablet' to Henry made by Joseph Wilton, who made the stagecoach for the coronation of George III. John Flaxman carved a beautiful relief in a small monument to Sophia Hoare, Henry's daughter. The relief shows mourners beside a dead body, but you cannot see the head, as it is obscured by grieving figures!

Below a stained glass window made by John Hayward, with *grisaille* portraits of Dr Johnson and Samuel Boswell and one of the Master of Revels to Elizabeth I – Edmund Tylney (d. 1610) is a small triptych icon of St Leonard (d. 559CE, patron saint of prisoners and Abbot of a monastery in Limoges) with St Laura and a prisoner (Leon Liddement, 1998). St Laura, from Cordoba, became an Abbess. But she was thrown into a cauldron of molten lead by Moorish conquerors in 864. Like many martyrs, she is seen with a martyr's cross.

Address Tooting Bec Gardens, SW16 1HS, +44 (0)208 769 1216, www.stleonard-streatham.org.uk | Getting there Mainline to Streatham (Thameslink and Southern), Streatham Hill (Southern), Streatham Common (Southern); bus: 50, 57, 109, 118, 133, 159, 201, 249, 250, 255, 315, 319, 333, G1 or P13 | Hours Sat–Thu 11.30am–2pm | Tip You might like to visit Tooting Bec Lido. First opened in 1906, it is the largest fresh water swimming pool in the UK.

101__ St Bartholomew

An Impressionist church

Built between 1827 and 1832 by the architect Lewis Vulliamy (1791–1871) in the neo-Gothic style; the church is large and spacious and has a timbered roof over the nave.

The church was the subject of a painting (*The Avenue, Sydenham*, 1871, National Gallery) by the Impressionist painter Camille Pissarro, who lived in London from 1870 to 1871 and who also painted the church of St Stephen, Dulwich (see ch. 88).

Of note inside the church is the *reredos* at the high altar, made and decorated from 1901 by an artist called Henry Wilson (1864–1934) who carved as the central panel a wooden painted *Adoration of the Magi*. This is a graceful and elegant composition of figures – some standing, some kneeling and sitting, producing a work of enormous variety. What is particularly striking is that behind the three kneeling kings (one of whom is opening a casket so that Jesus can see inside!), are a group of people, including an angel who takes the hand of one person behind. Here is a panel of the people for the people and some of them are even children. Behind there is also a shepherd with his sheep while another man brings in some pigeons. On either side of the panel are carvings of the four archangels. Wilson worked with John Dando Sedding at Holy Trinity, Sloane Street (see ch. 86). Not only was he a sculptor, but he was also a designer, architect and jeweller. He even designed the bronze doors for the cathedral of St John in New York. All around the church above the clerestory windows are some small stained glass roundels depicting the symbols of the Passion. Vulliamy's brother, Benjamin Lewis (1780–1854), made the clock for the tower and was the clock maker to both George IV and Queen Victoria. Allegedly the brothers had a falling out and the work they did on the church together was one of the last times that they were in a working partnership.

To the left of the church is a blue plaque to George Grove (1820–1900), author of the *Grove Dictionary of Music*.

Address 4 Westwood Hill, SE26 6QR, +44 (0)208 699 4817, www.stbartschurchsydenham.org | **Getting there** Train to Sydenham (Southern), Sydenham Hill (Southeastern); bus: 3, 363 or 450 | **Hours** Morning prayers 8.30am, Sat 9–11.30am, Sun service 8am & 10am; for details of other church openings and events, see website | **Tip** A 15-minute walk will bring you to Crystal Palace Park, with its Italian Terraces, maze and dinosaur sculptures.

102 St Giles-in-the-Fields

Protection for the poor and leprous

Here we are a stone's throw from Charing Cross Road and Oxford Street, but when Matilda, the wife of Henry I constructed a hospital for lepers here (1101), the site was surrounded by fields. A cup of charity was given to those condemned as they entered, a way of sanctifying them, on their way to be beheaded at Tyburn, the name of a village where Marble Arch is today, and which is associated historically with capital punishment. As was the norm for monastic and charitable institutions, Henry VIII closed the hospital in 1539. A new church was built from 1630 and then continued by Henry Flitcroft (1730–34), a Palladian architect who designed many country houses. It is thought that what we see today is broadly similar to how the building looked after its completion in 1733.

There were also gallows in the churchyard and one of the last to be executed here were Anthony Babington and 13 conspirators hanged for trying to assassinate Queen Elizabeth I (1586). The church has a poignant setting, as there were many burials here from a plague between 1592 and 1646. George Chapman who translated Homer's *The Iliad* and *The Odyssey* (1616) is buried here, and you can see a memorial to him in the church. Also look out for a memorial to the poet Andrew Marvell (1621–78), also buried here, a resident of the neighbourhood. John Milton's daughter was baptised here in 1647. And the list goes on… There is also a pulpit in the church, which used to be in West Street Chapel, from where John and Charles Wesley preached. Charles (1707–88) is well known as the author of many hymns.

You will notice the church's unified and coherent space. That is because although the pews provide a sort of structure, you are looking at a space that is not divided into a nave and side aisles. So your eyes are led straight towards the altar, and the boards of the Ten Commandments above.

Address 60 St Giles High Street, WC2H 8LG, +44 (0)207 240 2532, www.stgilesonline.org |
Getting there Tube or Crossrail to Tottenham Court Road (Central and Northern Lines);
bus: 1, 38 or 176 | **Hours** Mon–Fri 8.30am–5pm & Sun service times: 11am & 6.30pm
Evensong | **Tip** Right beside the church is a garden devoted to nature, where you can sit and
look at the spire of St Giles.

103 St Mary

Plague pits and ancient slabs

An ancient wooded parish and once long ago a village nearly 8 miles (13 kilometres) away from London, in the county of Essex. The name Walthamstow comes from 'Wilcumestowe', a place where strangers are welcome, so in keeping with the Christian tradition of offering hospitality. The ancient feel is notable in the churchyard straddled by a pathway going north to south and used as a walkway.

Here, the graveyard, broken up east and west by the path, is an eloquent elegy to extinction. The gravestones are so old that if there had once been inscriptions, they are not visible now. In a once relatively prosperous area, behold the graves of the unknown. But what size and bulk about the stones that carry them, affordable only by the historic elite of the parish. Note the slab coverings for the tombs. They appear to be so ancient that some of them have been pushed out of the earth and are ranked up precariously abutting the space above and the chill of the dead air. Don't be too put off though. The church possesses real charm.

William Morris (1834 – 96), the great Victorian visionary and designer lived nearby as a boy and was baptised in the church. He used to spend a lot of time in the woods not far from here at Epping Forest, learning all about wood and the crafts of wood as well as studying the birds, trees and plant forms that are central to so much of his decorative work.

Nearby are the Monoux Almshouses. They are so named in tribute to George Monoux (c. 1465 – 1544) a local resident, merchant and once Mayor of London who contributed to the rebuilding of the church in the 16th century.

Just beside the church is Vinegar Alley. Yes, vinegar really does have a local history here; it was used as some sort of desperate measure against the plague. The church had two plague pits nearby: one from the Black Death and one from the Great Plague of 1665.

Address 8 Church End, E17 9RJ, +44 (0)208 520 1430, www.walthamstowchurch.org.uk | Getting there Tube or Overground to Walthamstow Central (Victoria Line); bus: 69, 212 or W16 | Hours Only during service times (check website) | Tip Visit the William Morris Gallery, once his childhood home, in nearby Forest Road (www.wmgallery.org.uk). Also, the delightful Vestry House Museum (www.vestryhousemuseum.org.uk).

104 All Saints

A neighbourhood church

The church of All Saints is on the busy Wandsworth High Street. But when it was built, it would have been like an elegant parish church in a desirable residential area of London. Note some elegant buildings all around. The building is reasonably large and is made of yellow London brick with a mini version of a classical temple portico, complete with pediment. The white dressed tower makes the church stand out against all the shop fronts, which were once beautiful specimens of Georgian architecture. Inside is a large barrel vault presiding over a capacious interior with benched, box pews, reminiscent perhaps of how this would have been a local church for families and communities of Wandsworth.

There is a fascinating memorial revealing just how many local landowners and benefactors contributed to local religious culture and belief in the history of London. The memorial is a round headed classical arched structure, with antique decoration and some colouring. A nice comfortable setting for the person being remembered. He is dressed in a black robe falling to the ground and lined with a gold border. He is kneeling in front of a small lectern, hoping to secure himself a place in Heaven. The long inscription was presumably designed to explain the reason for this commanding memorial. For he was Henry Smyth, alderman of London (d. 1627), who bequeathed a sum of money of £1,000 to several towns in Surrey (including Wandsworth as it was not London then), for *y reliefe and setting the poor people…*

And another memorial illustrates the same relationship between benefaction in the earthly world and the desire to be committed to posterity. Susanna Powel was the daughter of Thomas Hayward of Wandsworth, a Yeoman of the Guard, and she was wife 'unto' John Powel of Wandsworth, servant of Queen Elizabeth and King James. She died in 1630, but left money and bread for 24 poor widows.

Address 98 Wandsworth High Street, SW18 1EP, +44 (0)208 788 4606, www.wandsworthparish.co.uk | **Getting there** Mainline to Wandsworth Town (South Western); bus: 39, 87 or 156 | **Hours** Daily 8am–6pm | **Tip** The church is situated close to the River Thames and the Ship Inn, a lovely pub beside the river.

105 _ Quaker Meeting House
Space, silence and simplicity

It is best to view this building from the other side of the busy Wandsworth High Street. From this vantage point you can see an elegant building that looks like a small manor house rather than a place for religious worship. In a sense, the architectural appearance is not surprising, as this is a Quaker Meeting House, not a church as such and a place that represents another form of dissenting practice that has its roots in the 17th century. And, unlike a church, generally a meeting house does not stand out with a steeple or a tower.

You will also see that the entrance is to the left of the building and not in the centre. Wandsworth had a special place for non-conformist practices of worship, and some say this is the oldest meeting house in London.

The property was originally endowed by a local woman called Joan Stringer, who had a small house, shop and three sheds, which she 'underleased' to the *Society of Friends* in 1674. In the burial ground of the house, you can see an inscription stone to her. Here, meetings rather than services happen, where people can sit in silence in a room, often with no other visual distractions or accessories. The customary reliance in most Protestant and Anglican churches on fabric and furnishings contrasts with the simplicity of the meeting house. The room is plain and restful, consisting of simple wooden benches arranged so that there is a sense of a middle space, or an empty space in the room. There might be a table with a book or a vase of flowers on it, or there might just be a plastic bag on the floor – the point being that in a purely communal way, we can come together to sit in a room.

There is silence, but voice can break into that too. Quakerism is democratic, in the sense that there is no call and response from a priest. People participate doing the same thing and this is reflected in this rather lovely building.

Address 59 Wandsworth High Street, SW18 2PT, +44 (0)207 228 1462, www.wandsworthquakermeeting.org | **Getting there** Mainline to Wandsworth Town or Clapham Junction (many lines); Tube to Clapham Junction (Northern Line); bus: 28, 37, 39, 44, 87, 156, 170, 220, 270 or 337 | **Hours** View the exterior. Interior if a meeting is on: Sun at 10.30am or the 2nd Tue in the month 12.30 – 1pm. The house is open on Open House weekend in September | **Tip** The church is located close to All Saints on Wandsworth High Street (see ch. 104) and is not that far from the River Thames.

106__ St Mary the Virgin
Elegant classical for the locals

The present church was designed by Thomas Hardwick (1752–1829). He is known to have advised Turner to stick to painting rather than architecture. The church dates to 1790, so it is contemporary with many of Hawksmoor's churches such as his wonderful St George's Bloomsbury (see ch. 10). This church has an elegant classical façade with Doric columns. And on top is a glorious little bell turret with classical columns. The church is white and makes a striking contrast against the green and the trees of the very old graveyard.

One of the distinguishing features of the interior are the high-box pews, which look compact and complete and give such an insight into how worship happened in family units or groups then. It would have been so easy to sneak in picnics, brandy and non-religious reading material. Sometimes they are used for displays; for example, hessian sacks, looking a little out of place, but which are actually propping up some plastic cut-outs of soldiers to commemorate old wars. But the actual space, sweeping down towards the high altar area painted light lemon and yellow, approached by a fine white row of Corinthian columns is nothing but majestic. It really is gorgeous.

And then there is the utterly OTT monument right beside the altar to Sir Josiah Child (1699). Not only does he adopt a swaggering stance, but clearly he is remembering his ancient Roman Emperor forebears. Except his hairstyle is more Georgian and ridiculous than it is Roman. But from a locals' perspective, he had to look the part, for he was the local landowner, having bought Wanstead House and becoming an MP.

The other highlight, which has caused a stir in art historical circles, is the picture of the *Entombment of Christ* by Il Guercino (1591–1666), hitherto thought to be a copy, but recently it has been discovered to be an original. I dread to think what the insurance for the church must be now!

Address Overton Drive, E11 2LW, +44 (0)208 530 8743, www.wansteadparish.org | Getting there Overground to Wanstead Park; Tube to Wanstead (Central Line); bus: 66, 108 or 308, W12 and W14 | Hours Mon–Fri 9–11.30am; Open Days every 3rd Sat of the month, or on a Sun for a service | Tip A 12-minute walk north from here will take you to Christchurch, Wanstead, built as a chapel at ease to St Mary.

107__St Mary the Virgin

A light interior perfect for a Hans Feibusch mural

By the time you have finished browsing through this book, you might just be a Hans Feibusch fan. Do go to this church (begun in 1954 by Thomas Ford) for another sublime mural by him – and another *Ascension*. This is the Christian event when we see Christ as he ascends to Heaven. Look at that figure kneeling beneath the great event that is unfolding, with one hand raised to his nose, while his left hand faces downwards. His body language is one of disbelief, almost loathing. And you will also see that Mary is the only figure actually looking out, when quite often she is seen to be shy and retiring. The Apostles are muscly; loosely draped, revealing flesh, while kneeling and facing him, showing us the soles of their feet. Feet are notoriously difficult to paint. Here is an artist who does not shy away from them.

The church is red brick, with a recessed arch, decorated with scenes of the Virgin's life. A type of painting known as *graffito* was used, in appearance like an Italian fresco. Also inside are some charming, quaint, unusual paintings of the *Old Testament* in little insets in the arches on the side aisles. These are painted by Clare Dawson, a relatively unknown, but evidently talented artist, who also executed the stained glass in windows by the altar. These depict subjects that find a way to connect events in the *Old Testament* with the *New Testament*. Here, the bestowing of the biblical seed for humanity down the generations from Moses to Abraham to David, and eventually to Adam and with Christ as the ultimate (although he was, as far as we know, never a seed sower – he just preached about it). These scenes are unusually placed, but all the same eye-catching.

The church has a clean ascetic. How it must have seemed like a fresh newly grown verdant meadow in the face of 1950s brutality, misery and austerity post-war.

HYMNS
636
437
448
374
137

Samuel anointed David in the midst of his brethren

Address Wickham Street, Welling, DA16 3QU, +44 (0)208 856 8221, www.stmarythevirgin.net | **Getting there** Mainline to Welling (Southeastern); bus: 89 or 486 from North Greenwich | **Hours** Wed 10am – noon and service times | **Tip** You can also visit the Greek Orthodox Church of Christ the Saviour in Upper Wickham Lane, where horses graze in a field nearby, which contains wall paintings from the 13th century.

108__ St Matthew

A naked mother and child

St Matthew's is in the heart of Westminster in Great Peter Street, so named after the patron saint of Westminster Abbey. In the 19th century, the area, known as the Devil's Acre, was a den of poverty and iniquity. Politicians must pass by the building constantly. The church caters well for them with free lunchtime organ recitals, while all around are statues, figurines, faces in corbels, blind screens, crosses in the wainscoting, an ornate altar, and Victorian decoration, made in their idea of the medieval. Built between 1849 and 1851 by George Gilbert Scott; there is a Lady chapel upstairs designed by Ninian Comper.

To enter, walk through a charming and unusually shaped vestibule, containing a liturgical chest and a cosy waiting room-like area.

In the cold bleak winter sits a naked woman and, on her lap, she holds and tries to protect a cold and naked baby. Here is an unusual sculpture of the Madonna and new-born Child, made by the contemporary sculptor, Guy Reid (2000) from carved lime wood. The roughly carved figures are bereft of the gold, kings, gifts, shepherds and the swaddling clothes we associate with the Virgin Birth. True to the bare essentials of the *Gospels of St Luke* and *St Matthew* that describe the birth of Christ, this image amplifies not only the brevity that narrates for the Christians the most important birth of all; but in its bareness shows the true reality of how Christ came into the earthly world. At a time where we are surrounded by constant and colourful visualising, how refreshing it is to approach the mother and child in this way. Here, though, baby Jesus is up, awake and eager to commence his special life. He looks ready to scramble off his mother's lap and go – sooner than most babies would.

You might like to look the *Road to Calvary* sculptures by Joseph Cribb (1892–1967), a pupil of Eric Gill, who worked with him at Westminster Cathedral.

Address 20 Great Peter Street, SW1P 2BU, +44 (0)207 222 3704, www.stmw.org | Getting there Tube to Westminster (Circle, District and Jubilee Lines); bus: 88, 211 or 507 | Hours Mon–Fri 8.30am–6pm | Tip The church is a 5-minute walk from Westminster Abbey and you can also visit St John's Smith Square, the location for regular classical music concerts.

109_ St George-in-the-East
Nature and mortuaries

From afar, St George looks like a castle, with towers and a tall commanding turret, which the illustrious 18th-century architect, Nicholas Hawksmoor (1661–1736) made to look like a rather large pepper pot. This church was designed to stand out; it is majestic, it is soaring – as was his key desire for any church, and it serves to dominate, despite being on such a busy road. You only need to look at Christchurch Spitalfields and St George (see ch. 10) and you will see how he fulfilled his quest for what a church should be and look like. St George's was ravaged inside in 1941 (it was completed in 1729). Here is a modern solution to the damage that was caused. You enter the church from the west (approached from the busy highway). You enter through a door, but instead of finding yourself in the interior, you go into what is basically a courtyard where straight ahead is a modern round arched window that becomes another west end, but which is glass filled and thus transparent. And although you still get a sense of the old Greek cross plan (a great favourite of Hawksmoor), the church does have a modern aesthetic.

Some of the windows are characteristic Hawksmoor – round headed, keystoned, tall and shapely. Then there are the keystones that drop, the circular or oval apertures that radiate light, and the solidity of elegance and the circulation of rhythm that make his churches so fine and memorable.

The church is situated in an area of London that has a rich history, where poverty and new industries went together. For example, this was the newly established 19th-century Docklands area, to produce wool and tobacco and where sugar refining was established (with 1,000 immigrant workers from Germany).

You can see the old mortuary to the church, which in 1904 became a mini natural history museum, visited by many children until World War II when it was forced to close.

Address 14 Cannon Street Road, E1 0BH, +44 (0)207 481 1345,
www.stgeorgeintheeast.withtank.com | Getting there Overground or DLR to Shadwell;
bus: 25 or 254 | Hours Daily, during normal working hours | Tip The church is located
10 minutes' walk from Wapping, an interesting area to wander around in, and the famous
Prospect of Whitby pub.

110_ St Winifrede

Running water in a stunning work of art

St Winifrede's is a bright, colourful and spacious church space, at one end of a residential street. The church is dedicated to a female saint called Winifrede who was born c. 600CE at Holywell in Wales. Urged by her parents to fear God, her wish to enter the church was not that easy. For Caradoc, the son of a prince, was obsessed with her, and while Winifrede tried to flee, he beheaded her outside church. A well sprang up at the spot where her head had landed. St Beuno discovered the severed head and placed it back with the body, covering it up with his cloak. Miracle of miracles, like Sleeping Beauty, Winifrede awoke and, for his sins, Caradoc was swallowed up by Heavenly forces. Thereafter she became a Holy abbess and built a healing well.

The church's ancient dedication meets the modern in a stunning painting by London-based artist Kate Wilson. Religious art is alive and well in many London churches, which provide fantastic locations for contemporary artists. In a side chapel, turned baptistry, full of statues, stations of the cross, radiators, pews, candles, a font and a red-brick wall, her horizontal painting rich with deep blue represents the baptismal waters. This is a bold image devoid of the figures you might expect to see: John the Baptist and Christ. While she paints water, at the heart of Baptism, the artist was not imagining the River Jordan, but based her work on studies of water at the River Wandle, a river that flows through Wimbledon and joins the Thames at Wandsworth.

The artist also imagined the flow of the river reflecting our journey through life. Sometimes calm, sometimes turbulent, the water flows on past green grass banks and small white flowers. Here, she was influenced by memories of C. S. Lewis' 'Wood between the Worlds' in *The Magician's Nephew* where everything grows so lusciously. The flowers, too, recall the beauty of the Garden of Eden.

Address 2 Latimer Road, SW19 1EP, +44 (0)208 542 1600, www.winefridechurch.co.uk | Getting there Mainline to Wimbledon (South Western Railway); Tube to Wimbledon (District Line), South Wimbledon (Northern Line); tram to Wimbledon from West Croydon; bus: 57, 93, 131 or 219 | Hours Daily during normal working hours | Tip Wimbledon town centre and Wimbledon village are very close by.

111__St George – Royal Garrison

Mosaics of a warrior saint

How fitting that a church dedicated to St George, the military saint who rescues princesses from nasty dragons, should be the name of this church, constructed 1862–63 on the orders of Lord Sidney Herbert, Secretary of State for War. So popular is St George that he is the patron saint of many cities and many countries. His story comes from a wonderful primer that artists in the medieval and Renaissance periods used to assist them in their work. This is *The Golden Legend*, written by the 13th-century archbishop of Genoa, Jacobus da Voragine. While his compilation of stories has legendary status, he would have drawn on earlier texts that trickled down the centuries, which perhaps got ever more elaborate as they continued to be told.

There is a clear and simple message with St George: trampling the dragon was a way to say that Christianity was there to stay against all powerful and evil forces. And he is never very far away from his armour or his sword. The church had a very specific purpose and that was to provide for the moral well-being of soldiers, whose physical and psychological well-being, it was thought, had been neglected.

The Wyatt brothers – Thomas Henry and Matthew Digby – were the architects in charge. If you look at the apse at the east end, you will see brickwork redolent of many Venetian churches. Indeed, the mosaics were done by the Salviati workshop from Venice (work also in the lobby of the House of Commons and Westminster Cathedral).

The church was partially destroyed by bombs in both world wars. In recent years, though, a restoration programme has begun. Note the Prussian blue iron gate, with the poppy, the UK's remembrance flower, the cornflower, for France and the forget-me-not for Germany, made to look as though they grow from the roots of the gate and where the gilded bird might just as well be singing.

Address Grand Depot Road, SE18 6XJ, +44 (0)208 858 1185, www.stgeorgeswoolwich.org |
Getting there Mainline to Woolwich Arsenal (Southeastern); DLR or Crossrail to Woolwich
Arsenal; bus: 122, 161, 178, 244 or 469 | **Hours** May–end Oct Sun 10am–4pm, Nov–end Apr
Sun 10am–1pm | **Tip** The church is opposite the beautiful Royal Artillery Barracks. Also nearby
is the church of St Mary by the river and the Woolwich New Wine Church.

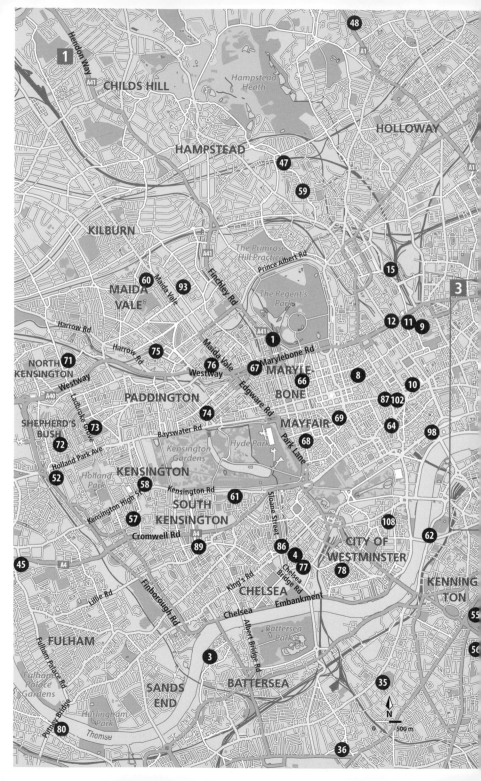

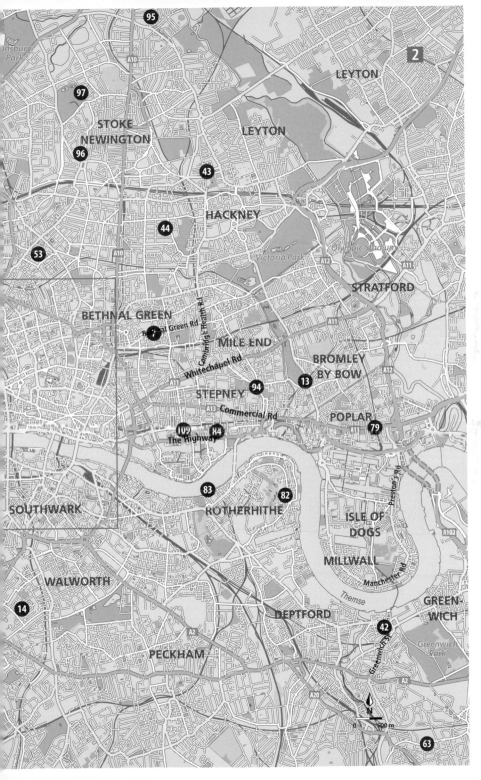

John Sykes, Birgit Weber
111 Places in London
That You Shouldn't Miss
ISBN 978-3-95451-346-8

Nicola Perry, Daniel Reiter
33 Walks in London
That You Shouldn't Miss
ISBN 978-3-95451-886-9

Kirstin von Glasow
111 Gardens in London
That You Shouldn't Miss
ISBN 978-3-7408-0143-4

Ed Glinert, Marc Zakian
111 Places in London's East
End That You Shouldn't Miss
ISBN 978-3-7408-0752-8

Julian Treuherz,
Peter de Figueiredo
111 Places in Manchester
That You Shouldn't Miss
ISBN 978-3-7408-0753-5

Julian Treuherz,
Peter de Figueiredo
111 Places in Liverpool
That You Shouldn't Miss
ISBN 978-3-95451-769-5

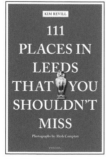

Kim Revill, Alex Compton
111 Places in Leeds
That You Shouldn't Miss
ISBN 978-3-7408-0754-2

Michael Glover,
Richard Anderson
111 Places in Sheffield
That You Shouldn't Miss
ISBN 978-3-7408-0022-2

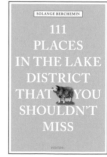

Solange Berchemin
111 Places in the Lake District
That You Shouldn't Miss
ISBN 978-3-7408-0378-0

Katherine Bebo, Oliver Smith
**111 Places in Poole
That You Shouldn't Miss**
ISBN 978-3-7408-0598-2

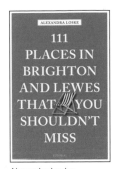

Alexandra Loske
**111 Places in Brighton
and Lewes That You
Shouldn't Miss**
ISBN 978-3-7408-0255-4

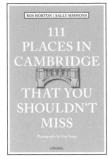

Rosalind Horton,
Sally Simmons, Guy Snape
**111 Places in Cambridge
That You Shouldn't Miss**
ISBN 978-3-7408-0147-2

Justin Postlethwaite
**111 Places in Bath
That You Shouldn't Miss**
ISBN 978-3-7408-0146-5

Tom Shields, Gillian Tait
**111 Places in Glasgow
That You Shouldn't Miss**
ISBN 978-3-7408-0256-1

Gillian Tait
**111 Places in Edinburgh
That You Shouldn't Miss**
ISBN 978-3-95451-883-8

Alexia Amvrazi,
Diana Farr Louis, Diane Shugart,
Yannis Varouhakis
**111 Places in Athens
That You Shouldn't Miss**
ISBN 978-3-7408-0377-3

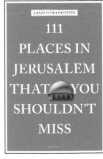

Laszlo Trankovits
**111 Places in Jerusalem
That You Shouldn't Miss**
ISBN 978-3-7408-0320-9

Kathleen Becker
**111 Places in Lisbon
That You Shouldn't Miss**
ISBN 978-3-7408-0383-4

Catrin George Ponciano
111 Places along the Algarve
That You Shouldn't Miss
ISBN 978-3-7408-0381-0

Andrea Livnat,
Angelika Baumgartner
111 Places in Tel Aviv
That You Shouldn't Miss
ISBN 978-3-7408-0263-9

Kay Walter, Rüdiger Liedtke
111 Places in Brussels
That You Shouldn't Miss
ISBN 978-3-7408-0259-2

Thomas Fuchs
111 Places in Amsterdam
That You Shouldn't Miss
ISBN 978-3-7408-0023-9

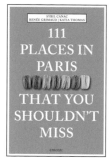

Sybil Canac, Renée Grimaud,
Katia Thomas
111 Places in Paris
That You Shouldn't Miss
ISBN 978-3-7408-0159-5

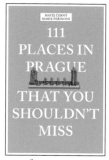

Matěj Černý, Marie Peřinová
111 Places in Prague
That You Shouldn't Miss
ISBN 978-3-7408-0144-1

Kai Oidtmann
111 Places in Iceland
That You Shouldn't Miss
ISBN 978-3-7408-0030-7

Jo-Anne Elikann
111 Places in New York
That You Must Not Miss
ISBN 978-3-95451-052-8

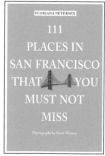

Floriana Petersen, Steve Werney
111 Places in San Francisco
That You Must Not Miss
ISBN 978-3-95451-609-4

I would like to thank Alistair Layzell who commissioned the book, Rosalind Horton for her careful, gracious and considerate copyediting and Laura Olk at Emons who answered many an email and was conscientiously 'present', doing the project management with such diligence. They were all very supportive in what felt like, at times, a very long list of churches to get through! There are two architect firms who have kindly agreed to let us use their own photographs to reproduce in the book: Roz Barr Architects for St Augustine's, Hammersmith and Theis and Khan architects for the Lumen Chapel. Andy Bowden supplied the photo for St Mary's, Harmondsworth; the image of St Stephen's, South Dulwich, was given by kind permission of the Vicar.

The University of Chichester agreed to let me use some text from the *Otter Memorial Papers* relating to the artist Hans Feibusch. Many church wardens and vicars have been incredibly kind in giving me tours of their churches and making suggestions to visit other churches, including Jack Stanley at St Saviour's, Eltham and for bringing home to me the plight of some of our churches; Tim Barnes, Glyn Williams and Simon Emdin, who also showed me a copy of a letter from Hans Feibusch; Father Henry Everett, the Reverends Jim Perry, Patrick Morrow, Erin Clark and Steven Tricklebank. The Reverend John Burniston was also very generous with his email time explaining various aspects of Anglicanism, as was Denis Pepper on the subject of St Botolph churches.

I would also like to thank Peter Gaskell for cartography, Edmund Flett for brainstorming a list of churches with me according to theme, Benedict Flett for doing the photography, Graham Barber for driving the photographer to some of the churches, Kay Barber for meals for weary churchgoers, Martin Amherst Lock for assisting with grammatical intricacies, David Shepheard for suggesting Notre Dame church, which, otherwise, I would have missed, and Alison Charles for advice on Netherlandish gables, and Lucy the cat sitting. Finally, thanks must go to the mini *A to Z*, who made the journeys using the black crosses that much easier.

Emma Rose Barber is an art historian who has been teaching art history to adults for many years. She has taken specialist study tours to Italy and the Netherlands and given lectures and tours in museums. She writes magazine articles on topics ranging from Bloomsbury bookplates and sacred clothing to the Romanian folk pocket. She is also writing a book on wayfaring.

Benedict Flett recently graduated from the University of Cambridge. He has been using a camera of some sort since he was young. He is interested in the correspondences between architecture and ideology and is documenting the 'regeneration' of inner London housing estates.